HOME MADE WINES & DRINKS

GAIL DUFF & VIC MORRIS

HAMLYN

Produced by New Leaf Productions

Photography by Mick Duff
Design by Jim Wire
Series Editor: Elizabeth Gibson
Typeset by System Graphics Ltd., Folkestone

First published in 1985 by
Hamlyn Publishing
Bridge House, 69 London Road
Twickenham, Middlesex, England

ISBN 0 600 32499 0

Printed in Spain

We would like to thank:
Valerie Clarke, Caroline Ward, Caroline Owens, Chris
Laing, Brian Cook and Son, Charing, Kent, Lurcocks of
Lenham, Lenham, Kent, Oast House Vineyards, Hardy
Street, Maidstone, Kent.

Larsa D. L. TF. 788 – 1985

NOTE

1. Metric and imperial measurements have been
calculated separately. Use one set of measurements
only as they are not equivalents.

2. All spoon measures are level unless otherwise
stated.

CONTENTS

INTRODUCTION

Over the past twenty years, home wine and beer making have become tremendously popular. By no means a new fad, this is really a return to old skills.

Until the end of the nineteenth century, home-made beer was the everyday drink for all the family; and if wine was drunk at all, it was that made by the housewife from home-grown and local fruits and vegetables. Then in 1881, a law was passed stating that no one without a licence could brew beer at home with an original gravity of over 1016. (*Original gravity* denotes strength; and considering that most brewery beers today have an original gravity of 1035–1040, one of 1016 would seem very weak indeed.) After 1881 brewery beer in the local public house thus became more popular; and home brewing declined considerably.

There was no law concerning country wines, but when between the wars women started to continue working after they were married, little time was found for such leisurely pursuits. The shortage of sugar during the last war must also have had some effect. The art of the wine maker was carried on by only a small number of enthusiasts.

When in 1963 the restrictions on home brewing were lifted, *beer making* became a popular hobby once again. Brewery beers were becoming more expensive and—before the Campaign for Real Ale was started—somewhat gassy and bland. What better than to have your own brew to offer to visitors or to sit down with it in the evenings instead of having to go out for a drink?

The new interest in beer making also revived the interest in *wine*. Home-made wine is now no longer something rather sweet and cloudy that Grandma used to make but something very drinkable that can be easily and expertly made in most home kitchens.

Successful brewing and wine making have been made more easy by the greater availability of ingredients and equipment. Though you can obtain all you need from chain stores and garden centres, you may prefer to buy from specialist home brewers' and wine makers' shops where there is usually a wider range. If you are a beginner, you can choose kits; if you are more experienced and feeling in need of a challenge, you can buy separate ingredients to make up your own recipes.

Another old-fashioned pursuit—carried out when there was a glut of fresh fruits—was the making of *fruit syrups* for use as drinks or for flavouring desserts and sauces. If you like the idea of fruit drinks that do not contain artificial colourings or flavourings, these are ideal. You will find, too, that *milk* is both nourishing and delicious and can be flavoured and served either chilled or warmed, as a thirst quencher, a nightcap or—when topped with ice cream—as a dessert. The increasingly popular *yoghurt* and the lesser known *buttermilk* can also be made into cool, refreshing drinks.

Mixing wines and beers to make *cold cups and punches* or heating them with spices to make *warming winter drinks* has always been popular for parties. *Cocktails,* however, are relatively new to Britain, though interest in them is growing fast. Surprise your friends by experimenting!

In the following pages, then, you will find instructions for making all these drinks. Whether you wish to turn your kitchen into a mini-brewery, to shake up a cocktail or whizz up a milk drink, this book should prove useful.

Note: Home Brewing and the Law

Although it is now perfectly legal to brew your own wines and beers to any strength, it is still against the law to sell them or even to use them as prizes in draws and competitions. Home distilling is against the law.

WINE

Making your own wine at home is much easier than you would at first think. The simplest way of all is to buy kits and grape concentrates from wine makers' suppliers, but once you have mastered the technique of using these, you will probably wish to experiment with the so-called *country wines* made from fruits, vegetables, flowers and herbs.

There are two essential qualities needed when making wine. The first is *cleanliness*. If your equipment is not properly cleaned and sterilised, you risk contamination; all your efforts to produce a good wine will have been in vain.

The second quality is *patience*. Although simple, the wine-making process is a lengthy one, and there is no way in which it can be hurried. The time that you actually spend working on the wine is quite short, but you may have to wait weeks or even months for it to clear or to stop fermenting. And even after if has been bottled there may well be another wait. When you first start to make wines, this waiting time may be irksome, but if you make a new wine every month there will always be something interesting to do. Once the first wine has been opened and savoured, you will never be without a drink to enjoy in the evenings or to offer to guests.

WINE-MAKING EQUIPMENT

Wine-making equipment is simple and relatively inexpensive but nevertheless essential if your brewing efforts are to be successful. Most items can be bought from the larger chemists, some chain stores, garden centres and health food shops and also from shops specialising in home-brewing and wine-making equipment and ingredients.

Even though some items such as measuring jugs, funnels and spoons are the same as those used in the kitchen, it is wise not to make do with your kitchen equipment. Keep a special set for wine making so that you will know that they will always be clean and available when you need them.

Boiling Pan: In order to boil enough water at once to make one batch of wine, you will need a stainless steel, enamel or aluminium pan which holds at least 4.5 litres/1 gallon of liquid. Other metals may give an unpleasant flavour to the water or leak out dangerous deposits. A pouring lip on one side of the pan will help when you are transferring the water to your fermentation bin, but it is not essential.

Fermentation Bin: In this container the wine undergoes its first fermentation. You will need two. Choose translucent or white polythene or polypropylene buckets, preferably with a tight-fitting lid. Rigid plastic buckets may give a plastic flavour, and colour or chemical may leak out from the coloured types. If you are making 4.5 litres/1 gallon of wine you will need two 9-litre/2-gallon buckets. If there is no lid, you can use a sheet of polythene tied round securely with string.

Special wine-making bins are available in 10-, 15- and 25-litre/2¼-, 3⅓- and 5½-gallon sizes. Some have tight-fitting lids with a hole in which to fit a fermentation lock; some have a tap fitted into the bottom for racking; others are simply plain.

Polypins—square, thin plastic containers fitted with a tap and put into a cardboard carton—are also available for wine making.

4.5 litre/1 Gallon Jars or Demijohns: From the fermentation bin, the wine is siphoned off into a 4.5-litre/1-gallon glass jar with a narrow neck that is known as a demijohn. You will need at least two of these since during the second fermentation the clear wine is siphoned off into a second jar. For fermenting, clear glass is best as it enables you to see when sediment has built up in the bottom of the jar. If you intend to make more wine while the first is still fermenting (the process may take several months), you will need more demijohns.

Siphon: For transferring the wine from the fermenting bin to the demijohn and from one demijohn to another, you will need a siphon. It is quite possible simply to use a 1.5-metre/1½-yard length of clear plastic tubing with an internal width of about 1cm/½ inch. However, since you wish to transfer as little sediment as possible into your clean jar, certain attachments will help to leave this behind.

The first is a J-shaped glass tube which fits on to the plastic tubing. The small upward hook is placed in the bottom of the jar, end pointing upwards away from the sediment.

The second is a piece of plastic tubing with 1-2 cm/½-¾ inch of the end blocked off. Above the seal are bored several holes which will let liquid through—but not the sediment.

You can also buy a siphon with a bellows mechanism that starts the flow of liquid, but this is not essential.

Bored Corks: These corks fit into the neck of the demijohn. They have a hole in the centre through which is inserted the fermentation lock (see below). To guard against their drying out, soak them in hot water before use, and again while you are racking the wine.

Rubber bungs are also available, but these often perish or—worse—stick fast to the neck of the jar. Use cork whenever possible.

Fermentation Lock: A fermentation lock fits through the hole in the bored cork. It is a simple device that allows gases to escape from the fermenting wine whilst keeping out air. Originally, all fermentation locks were made of glass, but now plastic ones are available.

The glass type consists of a tube going into an upward-facing loop. Into this loop is put a weak solution of sodium metabisulphite (see page 10).

While the wine is still fermenting, the levels of the solution in the loop are uneven. When fermentation is complete, they will become equal. This helps you to gauge when the wine is ready for racking or bottling. The drawback of these glass loops is that they are very fragile. To prevent their breaking it is easier to insert them into the cork before the cork is put into the jar. Use a twisting motion to ease them in and always hold them with a cloth in case they break in your hand.

Plastic locks are now available in a similar style. They are cheaper and far more durable as well as being able to help you check on the process of fermentation. On top of the loop they also have a large plastic cup which makes pouring liquids into the lock easier.

The other type of plastic fermentation lock consists of a small cylinder attached to a short tube. The sodium metabisulphite solution is put into the cylinder. Although this type is popular, it is not as easy with the loop type to see the air bubbles coming up through the liquid.

Whichever type of lock you use, insert a small piece of **cotton wool** in the top to keep out fruit flies.

Long-Handled Spoons: These are for stirring the wine while it is in the fermentation bin. You can use large wooden spoons, but sturdy plastic ones are easier to clean and sterilise.

Measuring Jugs: Use see-through types made of either plastic or Pyrex or those made of white or translucent polythene. For convenience, choose jugs of at least 600-ml/1-pint capacity.

Scales: These are essential for measuring ingredients. Choose ordinary kitchen scales fitted with a bowl rather than a tray. Make sure that the markings go down to at least 15g/½ oz as you will need only small amounts of some ingredients.

Polythene Funnels: You will need a large funnel for fitting into the top of the demijohn and a small one which fits into the neck of wine bottles. Choose funnels which have four small ridges round the outside of the neck. These will leave a small gap between the funnel and the jar or bottle, allowing air to escape. Without this air gap, the liquid will bubble up too much while you fill the jar or bottle.

Sieves and Strainers: During the wine-making process, the liquid has to be strained from the fruit or vegetable or other main ingredient. For this you will need either a large nylon sieve, a jelly bag or a large nylon straining bag. You can make one yourself by buying 2 metres/2 yards of nylon netting, folding it in half and sewing up the sides, or you can buy ready-made straining bags. You must also find some

method of suspending it over your fermenting bin or of fitting it round the rim of the bin. Some wine shops sell a strainer with interchangeable meshes that will fit over the rim of a specific bin.

Wine Bottles: You can buy bottles from shops which sell wine-making equipment, or beg them from friends, or from hotels, restaurants and even your local. Given a choice, many wine makers prefer clear bottles so they can check on the colour and clarity of their wine.

Long-Handled Brush: A wire-handled brush with stiff nylon bristles is essential for cleaning both wine bottles and demijohns.

Corks: Always buy new corks and, if the wine is to be kept for several years, buy the best quality. Soak corks in hot water for 30 minutes before use. Insert them into the bottles with the smooth end downwards.

Hand Corker: There are several different types. The simplest is a wooden cylinder and piston which you hit with a mallet. The advantage of the more sophisticated types is that they are quicker to use.

If you do not have a corker, push in the corks as far as possible by hand, then push them against the wall.

Plastic or Foil Caps: These fit over the top of the cork. They are not essential but give bottles a more professional appearance.

Labels: All wines should be labelled with the name, the date of making and of bottling and also with a reference number (see *Record Book* below). You can use the plain white stick–on labels available from most stationers or more attractive labels produced specially for wine bottles.

Record Book: Whenever you make wine, it will greatly help you to keep a record of such details as ingredients and method used, dates for adding the yeast, adding extra sugar, racking and bottling. You can use a plain notebook and devise your own system or use specially printed record books and cards which you can simply fill in and number. Keeping records will enable you to repeat your successes and also to improve on wines that do not come up to your standard.

Fruit Pulper: Use a fruit pulper to mash hard fruits and some berries. Find a stout piece of hard wood about 10 × 10 cm/4 × 4 inches and 1–1.5 metres/1–1½ yards high. Plane the top to smooth it so that it does not give you splinters, or alternatively, insert a horizontal handle through the top. Put the apples or other fruit into a large, plastic bin and stand the bin on a wooden board cut to fit inside the underneath rim of the bucket. Then simply pound your piece of wood up and down until the fruits are crushed to a pulp.

Press: A press can be used to extract juice from the harder fruits such as apples and pears, or from larger quantities of soft fruits and berries. Mechanical fruit presses are available. In comparison to most wine-making equipment they are expensive, but they will last for many years. They are not, however, essential for the beginner.

Thermometer: This is not essential for the beginner since it is fairly easy to determine blood heat by simply testing the water with your hand. However, if you find this difficult, special wine-making thermometers are available. They are large—about 30cm/12 inches long—and so easy to read and to handle. Most wine-making thermometers are filled with alcohol instead of mercury so that, should they break, they do no harm to the wine.

Hydrometer: Again, this is not essential for the beginner. It is used to gauge the sugar and alcohol content of the wine both while it is being made and after the fermentation process is complete. A chart and instructions for use are usually provided with this piece of equipment.

Vinometer: This is another small device which will help you to assess the alcoholic content of your wines. It is not essential and never very accurate, especially when you are testing wines that are on the sweet side.

CLEANING AND STERILISING

The essential factor when you are making wines is cleanliness. Make sure that the place where you are working is clean and dry, and sterilise all your equipment just before use.

The substance most used for sterilising winemaking equipment is *sodium metabisulphite*, more commonly known as *sulphite*. It is sold as crystals and as tablets (known as *Campden tablets*) which are more expensive. When dissolved in water sulphite gives off sulphur dioxide, a gas which will kill any unwanted yeasts, vinegar-producing bacteria and fruit flies.

To make an effective sterilising solution, dissolve either 15g/½oz sulphite crystals or 8 Campden tablets, plus 1 tsp citric acid; in 660 ml/1 pint water. A pungent gas will be given off, take care not to inhale it. This solution will stay effective for several hours and will be sufficient to clean all your wine-making equipment.

First make sure the equipment is clean and dry.

then pour the sulphite solution from jug to bin, to demijohn, swirling it round to clean every surface. Pour it through funnels and tubes and soak small items such as corks, bungs and straining bags in it for about 10 minutes. If wine has been spilt on work surfaces or the floor, these can be wiped with the same solution.

Any bottles or jars which have become discoloured can be soaked overnight in a weak solution of bleach or a substance called *Chempro* which can be bought from most wine makers' suppliers. Rinse them thoroughly with cold water after the solution has been poured out.

To sterilise a large quantity of wine bottles, wash them with hot water and then lay them on the oven rack in an oven preheated to 250°C/450°F Gas 8. Leave them for 15 minutes.

Wash all your equipment after use. Dry it, and put it away in a clean, dry cupboard.

WINE-MAKING INGREDIENTS

Water: All tap water contains chemicals such as chlorine and fluoride. When these chemicals are mixed with an acid, dangerous fumes may be given off; therefore, before any water is used in a winemaking process, boil it. It can be cooled to the correct temperature after boiling if necessary.

Yeast: Yeast is a living organism which grows and multiplies in the presence of sugar, converting the sugar to alcohol and carbon dioxide. It works best at a temperature of 18–23°C/65–75°F.

The ideal yeast for beginners to use is an allpurpose wine yeast. Brewer's or baker's yeasts will not produce enough alcohol. Yeast compounds are not necessary and may not be as effective.

Once you have successfully used an all-purpose yeast, you may like to experiment with yeasts which will give your wine the characteristics of commercial grape wines. A good wine makers' shop will sell a wide selection, including Burgundy, Bordeaux, Hock, Moselle, Sherry, Port and many others. Choose these yeasts carefully. It would be unwise, for example, to use a Hock yeast with a rich red wine such as elderberry, or a Burgundy yeast with one of the light flower wines.

Yeast Nutrient: In order to work properly, yeast requires minerals, vitamins and salts. These are found naturally in grapes, but when you are making wines from other ingredients they will be more successful if you add a little commercially prepared yeast nutrient. 1 teaspoon per gallon is usually enough, but always read the manufacturers' instructions to make sure.

Pectolase or Pectin-destroying Enzyme: Pectin is found in varying amounts in all vegetables and fruits. It is the substance which enables jam to set. In wine making, the presence of pectin is undesirable since it may cause wines to go cloudy and since it inhibits the amount of juice which can be extracted from the fruits. A pectic enzyme breaks down the pectin. It is marketed under various names including *Pectolase, Pectinase, Pectozyme* and *Pectolytic Enzyme,* and is available both as a powder and a liquid. Use the amounts recommended by the manufacturers'.

Acid: Fermentation of a wine is more effective if the liquid is slightly acid. Many fruits contain sufficient acid. Others such as bananas or peaches (as well as cereals, vegetables and flowers on which home-made wines are often based) need an added acid to aid fermentation and to provide a pleasant flavour. Lemon juice can be used, or citric, tartaric or malic acids, all available in powder form. For the amounts necessary see the following recipes, or read the manufacturers' instructions.

Tannin: Tannin gives wine a slightly astringent flavour. It also helps to clear it and improve its keeping qualities. Tannin occurs naturally in the skins of red-skinned fruits such as grapes, elderberries, blackberries and damsons. Apples, pears and gooseberries also have a sufficiently high tannin content. Wines made from other ingredients should have extra tannin added. The simplest way is to add 1 cup of cold, strong black tea per 4.5 litres/1 gallon liquid. Grape tannin or tannic acid can be bought in powder or liquid form from most wine makers' suppliers. For amounts to use refer to the manufacturers' instructions. Currants or raisins will supply extra tannin, as will the peelings from six medium-sized pears.

Body-Giving Ingredients: Extra ingredients may be added to some of the lighter flower and vegetable wines and to fruit wines such as strawberry to give body. Dried fruits such as raisins, currants or sultanas are the most popular body-giving ingredient. Some recipes use grape concentrate and others very ripe bananas. For the amounts to use refer to individual recipes.

Sugar: The best sugar for wine making is ordinary granulated white sugar, which is cheap, readily available and will not impart any additional flavour to the wine. Brown sugars will both colour and flavour wines. This is ideal if you are aiming for a sherry or Madeira, but not for most other wines. By the same token, golden syrup is not suitable. A set honey can be used sparingly but only when you wish to make a wine with the flavour of mead. Icing sugar, caster sugar, sugar lumps and preserving sugar are all more expensive than granulated and no more effective.

Invert sugar, specially produced for wine-making purposes, is sold by many wine makers' suppliers. It is more expensive than granulated sugar and you will need to use more per gallon. Invert sugar has been chemically broken down into glucose and fructose. The yeast can perform the same function on its own, but using invert sugar will speed up the fermentation process. If you wish, you can make your own invert sugar syrup and use it all throughout the process or simply for adding to the wine after racking (see basic method, p.13).

To make an invert sugar syrup: put 900g/2lb granulated sugar into a saucepan with 1 tablespoon citric or tartaric acid and 600ml/1 pint water. Bring them to the boil and simmer for 20 minutes. Cool, store in bottles and use when needed.

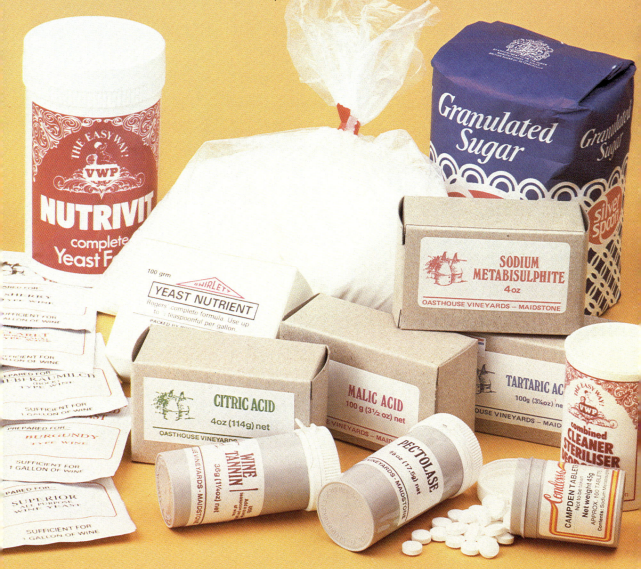

WINE KITS

If you are new to wine making, you might like to try making wine from a kit before attempting recipes for fruit, vegetable or flower wines.

A wine kit will provide you with a concentrated juice, yeast, nutrient and Campden tablets. These may simply be packed together in a box; or they come complete with bottles, syphons, corks, an airlock and sometimes even a demijohn all packed inside a fermenting bin.

There are four grades of wine kit. The most expensive—but the best as far as results are concerned—is known as the *Superior*. It includes a high quality concentrated grape juice with no artificial flavouring or other additives. No sugar is required when making up this kit. The *standard* kit provides concentrated grape juice that has been mixed with flavouring ingredients and usually some sugar. Extra sugar is usually needed for making the wine.

Budget kits may well contain a mixture of fruit juices plus sugar and flavouring. As with the standard kit, you will need extra sugar. *Express* wine kits may not contain any grape juice at all. Sugars and flavourings and sometimes other chemicals have been added. Again, you will need extra sugar.

If you would rather buy your ingredients sepa-rately, concentrated grape juice is available in tins from most wine makers' suppliers. Read the label before buying and to a certain extent be guided by price. The more expensive concentrates consist only of pure grape juice plus a little preservative. The cheaper ones contain a mixture of chemical additives, and the wine made from them will not be as good.

Each manufacturer recommends a slightly different method of making up their particular kit or concentrate, so read the instructions carefully. Basically, each method will follow the following lines:

1. Pour 2.25 litres/4 pints cooled boiled water into a demijohn.
2. Pour in the concentrate. Rinse out the container with more cooled boiled water and pour this into the jar.
3. Add sugar and yeast according to the manufacturers' instructions.
4. Fit an airlock.
5. Leave a jar in a warm place until fermentation stops.
6. Siphon the clear liquid into another jar. Add 1 crushed Campden tablet.
7. Leave the wine in a cool place for about 2 weeks or until clear.
8. Bottle and store for 2–3 months.

COUNTRY WINES

So called country wines can be made from fresh or dried fruits, flowers and herbs, vegetables and cereals.

There are three basic methods:

1. **The cold water method.** The ingredients are soaked in cold water for several days to extract the flavour. Campden tablets are added to prevent deterioration during this time. The yeast may be added 24 hours after adding the Campden tablets or towards the end of the soaking time. After soaking, the liquid is strained into a clean fermentation bin.

2. **Boiling the ingredients before adding the yeast.** This is not the most suitable method for fruit wines since it tends to make them hazy. It is, however, ideal for vegetables such as parsnips and potatoes which have to be softened. For method, see under specific recipes.

3. **Boiling water method.** This is the method used most frequently in the following recipes and the method is described in detail below.

1. Prepare your basic ingredient (fruit, flower, herb, cereal, vegetable) according to the instructions in the recipe.
2. Put the basic ingredient into the fermenting bin.
3. Add two-thirds the amount of sugar specified in the recipe.
4. Pour on boiling water.
5. Stir to dissolve the sugar. the mixture in the fermenting bin is now known as the *must*.
6. Cover and cool to lukewarm.
7. Add pectin-destroying enzyme. Leave in warm place for 24 hours.
8. Add yeast and yeast nutrient.
9. Cover and leave in a warm place for 3–4 days or until all the froth which at first forms on the top has sunk to the bottom. Stir every day during this period.
10. Strain the liquid into a second fermenting bin.
11. Siphon it into a demijohn. Fit a fermentation lock. Put into a warm, dark cupboard.
12. Leave the wine for 3 weeks, or until a thick sediment called the *lees* has formed in the bottom of the demijohn. The actual amount will depend on the basic ingredient. Bananas, for example, cause a great deal of sediment.
13. Siphon off the clear wine into a second demijohn. This is called *racking*.
14. Leave the wine for 2 weeks.
15. Rack again, letting the wine splash into the demijohn to aerate it.
16. Make the remaining sugar into an invert sugar syrup (see page 11).
17. Add one-third of the syrup to the wine.
18. If there is a gap at the top of the jar, top up with cooled boiled water.
19. Fit the fermentation lock and leave for 2 weeks.
20. Rack.
21. Taste the wine. Generally speaking, the drier it is at this point, the lower the alcholic content. If the wine is still on the dry side, add a further third of the syrup.
22. Fit the fermentation lock and leave the wine for 3–4 months or until it is completely clear.
23. Taste the wine. If the wine is still too dry, add the remaining sugar syrup and leave for a further 2 weeks. It is important not to add more sugar than the total amount specified in the recipe.
24. If the wine is to your taste, add 1 crushed Campden tablet per 4.5 litres/1 gallon. This will kill the yeast and prevent further fermentation. Leave the wine for 1 week.
25. Siphon into bottles and cork tightly. Leave the wine for at least 6 months before opening.

FRUIT AND BERRY WINES

Most fruits and berries can be used to make wines. They should be ripe but not overripe, with no bruises, blemishes or bad parts. Always use fruit when it is as fresh as possible. Remove all twigs, stalks and leaves.

Hard Fruits (Apples, Pears): Slice with a stainless steel knife. Pulp them before putting them into the fermentation bin.

Stone Fruits (Plums, Damsons, Peaches, Apricots, Cherries): Halve and stone the larger fruits, using a stainless steel knife. Put them into a fermentation bin and pour on the boiling water. When the must is cool, roll up your sleeves and squeeze the fruit by hand to a pulp. Crack the kernels of about 10 stones and add them to the must to give a slight almond flavour.

Soft Fruits (Raspberries, Strawberries, Black- and Redcurrants, Gooseberries, Blackberries): Pour on boiling water and squeeze with your hands when the must is cool.

Dried Fruits: Finely chop or mince.

Berries (Elderberries, Rosehips, Rowanberries, Hawthorn): Prepare elderberries in the same way as soft fruits. Pulp the rosehips, rowan and hawthorn berries.

Note: All the following recipes will make 4.5 litres/ 1 gallon wine.

APPLE AND RAISIN WINE

Use a mixture of cooking and dessert apples for this.

5.5kg/12lb apples
450g/1lb raisins
1.25kg/2½lb sugar
4.5 litres/1 gallon water, boiling
pectin-destroying enzyme
all-purpose yeast★
yeast nutrient

Chop and pulp the apples. Chop or mince the raisins. Put them into a fermenting bin with two-thirds of the sugar. Pour on the water. Cover and cool to lukewarm. Add the pectin-destroying enzyme. Leave in a warm place for 24 hours.

Proceed from step number 8 in the Boiling water method (p.13).

★*Alternative yeast:* Sauternes.

CRAB APPLE AND DATE WINE

2.75kg/6lb crab apples
1.8g/4lb pressed dates
100g/4oz raisins
900g/2lb sugar
4.5 litres/1 gallon water, boiling
 pectin-destroying enzyme
1 tea spoon citric acid
all-purpose yeast★
yeast nutrient

Chop and pulp the crab apples. Finely chop the dates and raisins. Put all these into a fermentation bin with the sugar. Pour on the boiling water. Cover and cool to lukewarm. Add the pectin-destroying enzyme and citric acid. Cover and leave for 24 hours.

Proceed from step number 8 of the Boiling water method (p.13).

★*Alternative yeasts:* Tokay, Sauternes.

GOOSEBERRY WINE

2.75kg/6lb ripe green gooseberries
250ml/8fl oz concentrated white grape juice
1.25kg/2½lb sugar
4.5 litres/1 gallon water, boiling
pectin-destroying enzyme
all-purpose yeast★
yeast nutrient

Top and tail the gooseberries. Put them into a fermentation bin with the concentrated grape juice and two-thirds of the sugar. Pour on the boiling water. Cover and cool to lukewarm. Using your hands, squeeze the fruit to a pulp. Add the pectin-destroying enzyme. Cover and leave for 24 hours.

Proceed from step number 8 in the Boiling water method (p. 13).

★ *Alternative yeast:* Chablis.

CHERRY WINE

2.75kg/6lb morello, red cooking cherries or
  black cherries
100g/4oz raisins
1.25kg/2½lb sugar
4.5 litres/1 gallon water, boiling
pectin-destroying enzyme
all-purpose yeast★
yeast nutrient

Remove the stalks from the cherries. Finely chop or mince the raisins. Put the cherries and raisins into a fermentation bin. Add the sugar. Pour on the boiling water. Cool to lukewarm. Using your hands, squeeze the cherries to a pulp. Add the pectin-destroying enzyme. Cover and leave for 24 hours.

Take out ten cherry stones. Crack them and extract the kernels. Add the kernels to the must. Add the yeast and yeast nutrient.

Proceed from step number 9 of the Boiling water method (p. 13).

★ *Alternative yeast:* Burgundy.

PLUM WINE

Use red–or purple-skinned plums for this recipe.

2.25kg/5lb plums
175g/6oz raisins
1.25kg/2½ lb sugar
4.5 litres/1 gallon water, boiling
pectin-destroying enzyme
all-purpose yeast★
yeast nutrient

Halve and stone the plums. Mince or chop the raisins. Put them into a fermenting bin with two-thirds of the sugar. Pour on the boiling water. Cover and cool to lukewarm. Add the pectin-destroying enzyme. Cover and leave for 24 hours.

Proceed from step number 8 in Boiling water method (p. 13).
★ *Alternative yeast:* Burgundy.

GREENGAGE WINE

Make as for Plum wine, using sultanas instead of raisins, and a Sauternes yeast. Add 175ml/6fl oz cold strong black tea with the yeast.

DAMSON WINE

2.75kg/6lb damsons (reserve 10 stones)
1.6kg/3½lb sugar
4.5 litres/1 gallon water, boiling
pectin-destroying enzyme
all-purpose yeast★
yeast nutrient

Put the damsons into a fermentation bin with the sugar. Pour on the boiling water and cool to lukewarm. Squeeze the damsons with your hands to reduce them to a pulp. Add the pectin-destroying enzyme. Cover and leave for 24 hours.

Take out damson stones. Crack them and take out the kernels. Add the kernels to the must. Add the yeast and yeast nutrient.

Proceed from step number 9 of the Boiling water method (p. 13).
★ *Alternative yeasts:* Port, Malaga.

BLACKBERRY WINE

2.75kg/6lb blackberries
225g/8oz raisins
1.6kg/3½lb sugar
4.5 litres/1 gallon water, boiling
pectin-destroying enzyme
all-purpose yeast★
yeast nutrient

Crush the blackberries. Chop or mince the raisins. Put them into a fermenting bin with two-thirds of the sugar. Mix well. Pour on the boiling water and mix again. Cool to lukewarm. Add the pectin-destroying enzyme. Cover and leave in a warm place for 24 hours.

Add the yeast and yeast nutrient. Stir well. Cover and leave for 3–4 days or until all the froth has sunk to the bottom.

Proceed from step number 10 of the Boiling water method (p. 13).

Note: To prevent the colour deteriorating, this wine should be kept in a dark place throughout the fermentation period and also after bottling.

★ *Alternative yeast:* Burgundy.

ELDERBERRY AND MALT WINE

1.8kg/4lb fresh elderberries, weighed with
  stalks; OR 450g/1lb dried elderberries
1.4kg/3lb sugar
450g/1lb malt extract
4.5 litres/1 gallon water, boiling
pectin-destroying enzyme
all-purpose yeast★
yeast nutrient
15g/½oz citric acid

Remove the fresh elderberries from their stalks. Put them into a fermentation bin. Add two-thirds of the sugar and all the malt. Pour on the boiling water and stir well. Cool to lukewarm. Add the pectin-destroying enzyme. Cover and leave in a warm place for 24 hours.

Add the yeast, yeast nutrient and citric acid. Stir well. Cover and leave in a warm place for 3–4 days, or all the froth has sunk to the bottom.

Proceed from step number 10 of the Boiling water method (p. 13).

★ *Alternative yeasts:* Burgundy, Port.

SEVILLE ORANGE WINE

This recipe is unusual in that no yeast is necessary and the ingredients used are very simple, It is a light, orange-coloured wine with a delicious marmalade flavour.

1.4kg/3lb Seville oranges
1.6kg/3½lb sugar
4.5 litres/1 gallon cooled boiled water
1 teaspoon yeast nutrient

Thinly pare the oranges and put the peel into a fermentation bin. Cut away and discard all the white pith. Holding each orange over a bowl, squeeze out as much juice as possible. Put the pulp that remains in your hand into the bin with the peel.

Put the sugar into another fermentation bin. Pour the orange juice over the sugar.

Pour 1.4 litres/2½ pints of the water over the peel ans pulp. Cover and leave for 24 hours. Strain the liquid into the bin containing the sugar and juice. Stir well.

Return the peel and pulp to the first fermentation bin. Pour on 900ml/1½ pints of the water. Cover and leave for 24 hours.

Strain the liquid again into the bin containing the sugar. Once more, return the pulp and peel to the first fermentation bin. Add 600ml/1 pint of the water to the pulp and peel. Cover and leave for 24 hours.

Strain the liquid again into the sugar. Return the pulp and peel to the first bin. Repeat this process, using 600ml/1 pint of the water, three further times. Stir the sugar syrup every day.

Add the remaining juice to the syrup. Stir well. Strain all the contents of the bin containing the syrup. Add the yeast nutrient.

Put the wine into a demijohn. Lightly cork it and leave it for 3 days. Seal it tightly and leave it for 9 months. Bottle and leave for at least 1 month.

ORANGE WINE

12 large oranges
4.5 litres/1 gallon water, boiling
450g/1lb raisins
1.4kg/3lb sugar
175ml/6fl oz cold, strong black tea
all-purpose yeast★
yeast nutrient

Set the oven at 190°C/375°F/Gas 5. Thinly pare 6 of the oranges. Put the peel on a baking tray. Put it into the oven for 20 minutes or until brown. Put the peel into a bowl. Pour on 1.15 litres/2 pints boiling water. Leave until the water is cold.

Squeeze the juice from all the oranges. Finely chop or mince the raisins. Put them into a fermenting bin. Add the sugar. Strain in the liquid from the orange peel. Add the rest of the boiling water and the tea. Stir well, cover and cool to lukewarm.

Add the yeast and yeast nutrient. Cover and leave for 8 days. Siphon into a demijohn and proceed from step number 10 of the Boiling water method (p. 13).

★ *Alternative yeasts:* Sauternes, Tokay.

BANANA WINE

1.8kg/4lb ripe bananas; or 675g/1½lb dried bananas
450g/1lb raisins
1.4kg/3lb sugar
4.5 litres/1 gallon water, boiling
1 Campden tablet
pectin-destroying enzyme
15g/½oz citric acid
all-purpose yeast★
yeast nutrient

Peel and mash the bananas. Chop about four of the least blemished skins. Chop or mince the raisins. Put all these into the fermenting bin. Pour on the water. Cover and cool to lukewarm. Add the Campden tablet, pectin-destroying enzyme and citric acid. Cover and leave for 3 days, stirring every day.

Strain the liquid into a second fermentation bin. Add the yeast and yeast nutrient.

Proceed from step number 9 of the Boiling water method (p. 13). After bottling, this wine should be kept for at least 18 months.

★*Alternative yeasts:* Tokay, Chablis.

DRIED APRICOT WINE

500g/1lb 2oz apricots
500g/1lb 2oz raisins
1.25kg/2½lb sugar
1 teaspoon citric acid
4.5 litres/1 gallon boiling water
pectin-destroying enzyme
all-purpose yeast★
yeast nutrient

Finely chop or mince the apricots and raisins. Put them into a fermentation bin with the sugar and citric acid. Pour on the boiling water. Cover and cool to lukewarm. Add the pectin-destroying enzyme. Cover and leave for 24 hours.

Proceed from step number 8 of the Boiling water method (p. 13).

★*Alternative yeasts:* Tokay, Sauternes.

RASPBERRY WINE

1.8kg/4lb raspberries
450g/1lb raisins
1.25kg/2½lb sugar
4.5 litres/1 gallon water, boiling
pectin-destroying enzyme
175ml/6fl oz strong, cold black tea
all-purpose yeast★
yeast nutrient

Crush the raspberries. Finely chop or mince the raisins. Put them into a fermentation bin. Add two-thirds of sugar. Pour on the boiling water. Cover and cool to lukewarm. Add the pectin-destroying enzyme. Cover and leave for 24 hours. Add the tea.

Proceed from step number 8 of the Boiling water method (p. 13).

★*Alternative yeast:* Bordeaux

REDCURRANT WINE

900g/2lb redcurrants
450g/1lb raisins
1.25kg/2½lb sugar
4.5 litres/1 gallon water, boiling
pectin-destroying enzyme
all-purpose yeast★
yeast nutrient

String and crush the redcurrants. Finely chop or mince the raisins. Put them into a fermentation bin. Add two-thirds of the sugar. Pour on the boiling water. Stir, cover and cool to lukewarm. Add the pectin-destroying enzyme. Cover and leave for 24 hours.

Proceed from step number 8 of the Boiling water method (p. 13).

★*Alternative yeast:* Burgundy.

ROSEHIP WINE

1.6kg/3½lb rosehips
225g/8oz raisins
1.4kg/3lb sugar
4.5 litres/1 gallon boiling water
pectin-destroying enzyme
all-purpose yeast★
yeast nutrient

Mince the rosehips and raisins. Put them into a fermentation bin, with two-thirds of the sugar. Pour on the water. Stir well, cover and cool to lukewarm. Add the pectin-destroying enzyme. Cover and leave for 24 hours.

Add the yeast and yeast nutrient. Cover and leave in a warm place for 10 days.

Proceed from step number 10 of the Boiling water method (p. 13), filling the demijohn only to the shoulder as the wine ferments vigorously.

★*Alternative yeast:* Sherry.

GRAPE WINE

6.75kg/15lb wine grapes
all-purpose yeast
Campden tablets

Crush the grapes. Put them into a fermentation bin. Add the yeast. Leave for 4–5 days or until the sediment (or crown) sinks to the bottom.

Strain the wine. Put it into a demijohn and fit the fermentation lock. Leave the wine until it clears.

Rack into another demijohn. Add 1 crushed Campden tablet per gallon. Leave for 1 week. Bottle.

Note: This makes a dry wine. If a sweeter wine is required, add an invert sugar syrup (see p.11) to taste after racking. Refit the fermentation lock and leave until the wine has fermented again. then rack and add the Campden tablet.

VEGETABLE WINES

Wines can be made from both root vegetables and from surface vegetables such as beans or pea pods. Those made from root vegetables tend to be richer.

Always use main crop root vegetables, preferably in the autumn and winter. Parsnips are definitely better if they have been left in the ground until after several frosts.

Root vegetables need little preparation. Scrub them well. Do not peel them but remove any blemishes or rotten parts. Then either chop or thinly slice them.

To extract the flavour from vegetables, boil them first in the specified amount of water until they are soft but still intact and not mushy. They contain no acid and so some must be added in the form of orange or lemon juices or citric or tartaric acid.

PARSNIP WINE

1.4kg/3lb parsnips
4.5 litres/1 gallon cold water
100g/4oz raisins, chopped or minced
1.4kg/3lb sugar
pectin-destroying enzyme
15g/½oz citric acid
all-purpose yeast★
yeast nutrient

Scrub and thinly slice the parsnips. Put them into a saucepan with the water. Bring them to the boil. Simmer, uncovered, for 20 minutes until tender but not mushy.

Put the raisins and two-thirds of the sugar into a fermentation bin. Strain on the liquid from the parsnips. Stir well. Cover and cool to lukewarm. Add the pectin-destroying enzyme. Cover and leave for 24 hours.

Proceed from step number 8 of the Boiling water method (p. 13).

★ *Alternative yeasts:* Sauternes, Tokay.

CARROT WHISKY

2.75kg/6lb carrots
4.5 litres/1 gallon cold water
450g/1lb raisins
2 oranges
2 lemons
450g/1lb wholewheat grains, crushed (see Grain Wines), (p. 28)
1.8kg/4lb sugar
pectin-destroying enzyme
all-purpose yeast
yeast nurient

Thinly slice the carrots. Put them into a large pan with the water. Bring them to the boil and simmer them for 25minutes or until they are tender but not over-soft.

Chop or mince the raisins. Thinly pare the rinds from the oranges and lemons. Cut away all the pith. Slice the flesh.

Put the raisins, orange and lemon rinds and flesh into a fermentation bin with the wheat and two-thirds of the sugar. Tip in the carrots plus the water. Stir well. Cover and cool to lukewarm. Add the pectin-destroying enzyme. Cover and leave in a warm place for 24 hours.

Stir in the yeast and yeast nutrient. Cover and leave in a warm place for 2 weeks, stirring every day.

Proceed from step number 10 of the Boiling water method (p. 13).

BEETROOT WINE

2.25kg/5lb beetroot
6 cloves
1 cinnamon stick
4.5 litres/1 gallon cold water
1.4kg/3lb sugar
pectin-destroying enzyme
juice of 1 lemon
all-purpose yeast★
yeast nutrient

Scrub and thinly slice the beetroot. Put it into a saucepan with the cloves, cinnamon and water. Bring it to the boil and simmer, uncovered, for 45 minutes or until tender.

Put two-thirds of the sugar into a fermentation bin. Strain in the liquid onto the sugar. Stir well and cool to lukewarm. Add the pectin-destroying enzyme. Cover and leave for 24 hours.

Add the lemon juice, yeast and yeast nutrient. Cover and leave to ferment for 3–4 days or until the crown (sediment) has sunk to the bottom.

Proceed as from step number 10 of the Boiling water method (p. 13).
★ *Alternative yeast:* Claret.

POTATO AND PRUNE WINE

1.4kg/3lb old potatoes
450g/1lb prunes, stoned and chopped
450g/1lb pearl barley
1.4kg/3lb demerara sugar
4.5 litres/1 gallon water, boiling
pectin-destroying enzyme
juice 2 lemons
all-purpose yeast★
yeast nutrient

Scrub and thinly slice the potatoes. Put them into a fermentation bin with the prunes, pearl barley and two-thirds of the sugar. Pour on the boiling water. Stir well, cover and cool to lukewarm. Add the pectin-destroying enzyme. Cover and leave for 24 hours.

Proceed from step number 8 of the Boiling water method (p. 13).
★*Alternative yeasts:* Tokay, Madeira.

FLOWER, HERB AND SPICE WINES

Flowers and herbs both from the garden and from the countryside make fragrant wines that will bring reminders of summer days. Pick them on a dry day, after the dew has dried but before the sun has become too hot. Do not keep them for any period in a polythene bag; always use them on the day that they are picked.

Many of the once most popular flowers for wines have become scarce in recent years. These include cowslips and primroses. If you wish to make wine from these, buy dried flowers from wine makers' suppliers and herbalists. Many other flowers and herbs—for example lemon balm, dandelions, and elderflowers— can be bought dried and are useful for winter wine making.

When using fresh flowers, remove all the stalks and green parts from the flower heads. Use only the leaves of herbs, discarding all the stalks.

Traditionally, herbs and flowers used for wine making are measured out in liquid measures, e.g. 1 pint rose petals.

Most spices are used in small quantities to flavour other wines (see Rice and Juniper page 29), but ginger can be used successfully as the main ingredient.

Flowers, herbs and spices will give flavour only. It is therefore necessary to use raisins or concentrated grape juice for body—also acid and tannin. A pectin-destroying enzyme is added to most of the recipes below to give the wine clarity.

ROSE PETAL WINE

2.25 litres/4 pints fresh sweet scented rose petals OR 50g/2oz dried
1kg/2lb 4oz sugar
500g/1lb 2oz raisins, chopped or minced
2 teaspoons citric acid
wine tannin according to manufacturers' instructions
all-purpose yeast★
yeast nutrient

Make as for elderflower wine (p.25).
★*Alternative yeast: Sauternes.*

DANDELION WINE

3.5 litres/6 pints dandelion flowers, fully open
4.5 litres/1 gallon water, boiling
450g/1lb raisins, chopped or minced
1.4kg/3lb sugar
2 teaspoons citric acid
pectin-destroying enzyme
175ml/6fl oz cold, strong black tea
all-purpose yeast★
yeast nutrient

Pick all the green parts from the dandelion flowers. Put the flowers into a fermentation bin. Pour the boiling water over them. Cover and leave for 3 days, stirring twice a day.

Put the flowers and liquid into a large pan. Bring them to the boil and boil for 10 minutes.

Put the raisins, two-thirds of the sugar and citric acid into a fermentation bin. Strain on the liquid. Stir well. Cover and cool to lukewarm. Add the pectin-destroying enzyme. Cover and leave for 24 hours.

Proceed from step number 8 of the Boiling water method (p. 13).

★*Alternative yeast:* Chablis

ELDERFLOWER WINE

fresh elderflower heads (see below) OR 25g/1oz
  dried elderflowers
1kg/2lb 4oz sugar
500g/1lb 2oz raisins, chopped or minced
2 teaspoons citric acid
wine tannin according to manufacturers'
  instructions
all-purpose yeast★
yeast nutrient

If you are using fresh elderflowers, shake the heads into a jug so the tiny florettes fall off. You will need a 600ml/1 pint measure of these florettes.

Put the florettes or the dried elderflowers into a fermentation bin with two-thirds of the sugar, the raisins, citric acid and tannin. Pour on the boiling water. Stir, cover and cool to lukewarm.

Add the yeast and yeast nutrient. Cover and keep in a warm place for 10 days, stirring every day.

Strain and put into a demijohn. Fit a fermentation lock.

Proceed from step number 12 of the Boiling water method (p. 13).

★ *Alternative yeast:* Champagne.

COWSLIP WINE

On no account should you go out picking cowslips for this wine. Dried cowslips are available from some winemakers' suppliers.

50g/2oz dried cowslips
2 oranges
1 lemon
1.8kg/4lb sugar
4.5kg/1 gallon water, boiling
pectin-destroying enzyme
175ml/6fl oz strong, cold black tea
all-purpose yeast★
yeast nutrient

Put the cowslips into a fermentation bin. Thinly pare the rinds from the oranges and lemons. Add them to the cowslips. Add the sugar. Pour on the boiling water and stir. Cover and cool to lukewarm. Add the pectin-destroying enzyme. Cover and leave for 24 hours.

Add the strained juices of the oranges and lemons, tea, yeast and yeast nutrient. Cover and leave for 10 days in a warm place, stirring every day.

Strain into a demijohn and fit a fermentation lock.

Proceed from step number 12 of the Boiling water method (p. 13).

★ *Alternative yeast:* Sauternes.

LEMON BALM WINE

600ml/1 pint lemon balm leaves
900g/2lb raisins
1.25kg/2½lb sugar
4.5 litres/1 gallon water
all-purpose yeast★
yeast nutrient
1 Campden tablet

Finely chop the lemon balm leaves. Chop or mince the raisins. Put the leaves and raisins into a fermentation bin. Pour on the boiling water. Cover and leave for 10 days, stirring every day.

Put all the sugar into a second fermentation bin. Strain on the liquid. Add the yeast and yeast nutrient. Cover and leave in a warm place for 2 weeks.

Strain the wine and put it into a demijohn. Fit a fermentation lock. Leave until fermentation is complete.

Rack into another demijohn. Add one crushed Campden tablet. Leave for 1 week. Bottle.

CARUM CARVI WINE

Carum Carvi is the Latin name for the caraway plant.

25g/1oz caraway seeds
1.15 litres/2 pints water
pectin-destroying enzyme
3.5 litres/6 pints cold, strong black tea
1.4kg/3lb sugar
450g/1lb raisins, chopped or minced
15g/½ oz citric acid
sherry yeast
yeast nutrient
1 Campden tablet

Put the caraway seeds into a saucepan with the water. Bring them to the boil and simmer for 15 minutes. Add the tea. Bring to the boil.

Put the raisins and sugar into a fermentation bin. Pour in the boiling liquid. Stir, cover and cool to lukewarm. Add the pectin-destroying enzyme. Cover and leave for 24 hours.

Add the citric acid, yeast and yeast nutrient. Cover and leave in a warm place for 1 week. Strain and put the wine into a demijohn. Fit a fermentation lock.

Leave until the fermentation process is complete. Rack into another demijohn. Add one crushed Campden tablet. Leave for 1 week. Bottle.

GINGER WINE

75g/3oz DRIED root ginger
4.5 litres/1 gallon water
1.4kg/3lb demerara sugar
225/8oz raisins
2 oranges
2 lemons
15g/½oz essence of cayenne
15g/½oz tartaric acid
175ml/6oz cold, strong black tea
all-purpose yeast★
yeast nutrient
1 Campden tablet

Put the ginger, water and sugar into a saucepan and boil them for 30 minutes. Cool to lukewarm.

Finely chop or mince the raisins. Thinly pare the rinds from the oranges and lemons. Strain the juices.

Put the raisins, fruit peels and juices, essence of cayenne, tartaric acid and tea, into a fermenting bin. Add the ginger in its syrup. Stir. Add the yeast and yeast nutrient. Cover and leave in a warm place for 10 days.

Strain. Put the wine into a demijohn and leave until the fermentation is complete.

Rack into another demijohn. Add one crushed Campden tablet. Leave for 1 week. Bottle.

Note: Essence of cayenne may be bought from most large chemists.

★ *No alternative yeast recommended.*

GRAIN WINES

The grains most used for wine making are wheat, barley, rice and maize. Buy them whole and unpolished from winemakers' suppliers or from health food shops. Before use they should be washed well in several changes of water to remove any toxic sprays, then coarsely crushed in a blender or food processor.

Grains contain a large quantity of starch but little natural sugar. It is therefore a good idea to use a special cereal yeast which will convert the starch to sugar. Yeasts which will give special flavours, such as sherry, may also be used.

Like herbs and flowers, grains themselves will not provide tannin or acid. Therefore add raisins or grape concentrate, lemon or orange juices or an acid and tannin or cold tea. The combination of grains and demerara sugar will make rich, dark coloured wines.

Grain wines usually take longer to ferment and mature than wines made from other ingredients.

WHEAT WINE

657g/1½lb whole wheat grains, crushed or cracked
657g/1½lb raisins, chopped or minced
1.4/3lb demerara sugar
4.5 litres/1 gallon water, boiling
7g/¼ oz citric acid
cereal yeast★
yeast nutrient

Put the wheat, raisins and two-thirds of the sugar into a fermentation bin. Pour the boiling water over them. Stir well. Cover and cool to lukewarm.

Stir in the citric acid, yeast and yeast nutrient. Cover and leave in a warm place for 3 weeks, stirring every day.

Strain the wine and siphon it into a demijohn. Fit a fermentation lock.

Proceed from step number 12 of the Boiling water method (p. 13).
★ *Alternative yeasts:* Sherry, Madeira.

Maize Wine

Make as for Wheat Wine, using 675g/1½lb maize.
★ *Alternative yeast:* Sauternes.

SPICED BARLEY WINE

675g/1½lb pot barley, crushed
6 cloves
6 allspice berries
675g/1½lb raisins
1.4kg/3lb demerara sugar
4.5 litres/1 gallon water, boiling
7g/¼ oz citric acid
cereal yeast★
yeast nutrient

Put the barley into a fermentation bin. Crush the cloves and allspice berries. Chop or mince the raisins. Add them to the barley. Put in two-thirds of the sugar. Pour on the boiling water. Stir well. Cover and cool to lukewarm.

Add the citric acid, yeast and yeast nutrient. Stir, cover and leave in a warm place for 3 weeks, stirring every day.

Proceed from step number 10 of the Boiling water method (p. 13).
★ *Alternative yeast:* Sauternes.

RICE AND JUNIPER WINE

1.4kg/3lb brown rice, long- or short-grain, crushed
10 juniper berries
225g/8oz raisins
1.6kg/3½lb sugar
4.5 litres/1 gallon water, boiling
7g/¼ oz citric acid
cereal yeast★
yeast nutrient

Put the rice into a fermentation bin. Crush the juniper berries. Chop or mince the raisins. Add them to the rice with two-thirds of the sugar. Pour on the boiling water. Stir well. Cover and cool to lukewarm.

Stir in the citric acid, yeast and yeast nutrient. Cover and leave in a warm place for 3 weeks, stirring every day.

Proceed from step number 10 of the Boiling water method (p. 13).

★ *Alternative yeast:* All-purpose.

CUMBERLAND BRANDY

Although the ingredients for this wine are very similar to the Wheat Wine (p. 28), it turns out richer and darker. It is excellent with Christmas Pudding.

900g/2lb whole wheat grains, crushed
900g/2lb raisins, chopped or minced
1.6kg/3½lb demerara sugar
4.5 litres/1 gallon warm water
juice 2 lemons, strained
cereal yeast★
yeast nutrient
1 egg white

Put the wheat, raisins and all the sugar into a fermentation bin. Pour on the water and stir well. Add the lemon juice, yeast and yeast nutrient. Cover and leave in a warm place for 2 weeks, stirring every day.

Strain into a second fermentation bin. Siphon into a demijohn. Fit a fermentation lock. Leave for 6 weeks or until fermentation is complete. Siphon off into bottles.

★ *Alternative yeast:* All-purpose, Madeira.

PROBLEMS AND REMEDIES

Stuck Fermentation: If the wine stops fermenting while it is still sweet and syrupy, this is called a stuck fermentation. It could have been caused by one of the following:

adding too much sugar at once

keeping the wine in too high or too low a temperature for the yeast to survive

using an unsuitable yeast or one that has been stored in poor conditions for too long a time

lack of a yeast nutrient

Remedies

1. Aerate the wine by splashing it from one demijohn to another. The extra oxygen which becomes absorbed in the wine may well start the yeast working again.

2. Add more yeast nutrient.

3. Move the wine to a cooler or a warmer place. If it has been in too cool a place, the yeast cells will have remained dormant and will only need a little warmth to start them working again. If the wine has been too hot, some of the yeast cells will have been destroyed. If only a few are lost, the yeast may start working again. If not, add more yeast, see below.

4. Add more yeast. This will be more effective if it has already started to ferment when it is added. First, dissolve 2 teaspoons sugar in 150ml/l/¼ pint warm water. Leave the solution to cool and put it into a sterilised bottle. Add ¼ teaspoon citric acid, and sufficient yeast and yeast nutrient for your volume of wine. Plug bottle with cotton wool and leave it in a warm place until the yeast is frothing vigorously. This may take a few days.

Put the frothing mixture into a demijohn with 600ml/1 pint of the stuck wine. Plug with cotton wool and leave in a warm place for a few days until the wine has begun to ferment. Add a further 600ml/1 pint of the wine and leave to ferment again. Add 1.15 litres/2 pints more of the wine. Leave for a few days again for it to start fermenting. Add the remaining wine and leave it to ferment out.

5. If you have added too much sugar to the wine at once, dilute the wine with cooled boiled water.

Vinegar Taste and Smell: If your wine smells and tastes of vinegar, it has probably been infected by the vinegar fly. There are four possible causes:

equipment was not properly sterilised

wine was left exposed to the air for too long during the racking process

no sulphite in the fermentation lock

liquid in the fermentation lock evaporated

Unfortunately, there is no remedy for vinegar infected wine. Most people throw it away, but try it

first since it can make exceptionally good wine vinegar.

Haziness: Most wine takes 2 months or longer to clear in the demijohn. If after about 12 weeks it is still cloudy or hazy, there may well be a fault. However, a sudden drop in temperature may help to clear a reluctant wine, so before you try any other remedies, place the wine in the refrigerator for a few days, and then rack it immediately it is clear. If this does not work, you will have to try other methods. There are several causes of and solutions to haziness in the wine:

1. You used copper, iron, tin or zinc equipment or lead-glazed earthenware vessels for fermenting. A haze brought about under these conditions will gradually increase as the wine matures. However, if spotted early it can be stopped from developing any further by adding ¼ teaspoon citric acid.

2. No pectin-destroying enzyme was added. A pectin haze can very often be removed by adding the enzyme to the wine in the demijohn. Take out 150ml/¼ pint of the wine. Mix in the pectin-destroying enzyme and stir until it has dissolved. Return the mixture to the wine in the demijohn and stir thoroughly. The sediment should settle within a few days.

3. A protein haze has developed. This can only be removed by the use of a wine filter or by adding finings to the wine. The use of finings is by far cheaper and easier. Special finings can be bought from winemakers' suppliers. Follow the manufacturers' instructions.

Red wines becoming brown and cloudy: If a red wine has become brown and cloudy it has either been exposed to the air for too long or has been placed in the light during fermentation or after bottling. Unfortunately the wine will be undrinkable. There is no remedy; all you can do is throw it away.

Flowers of Wine: White specks or a white skin forming on the surface of the wine are known as flowers of wine. They are caused by a type of wild yeast which can develop if the wine is exposed to the air. If they are allowed to remain, your wine will become watery and of low alcoholic strength. As soon as they become noticeable, skim them off by gently tipping the demijohn. Then add 2 crushed Campden tablets per 4.5 litres/1 gallon of wine.

If left to develop, the flowers of wine may well have made the wine undrinkable. Throw it away and thoroughly sterilise all your equipment.

Lack of Flavour. If your wine lacks flavour it may well be due to insufficient acid. This problem occurs more with the flower and grain wines. The best solution is to blend the wine with another that has a strong acid flavour.

Alternatively, citric acid may be added. Use only a very small amount at a time. Leave the wine to rest for about 30 minutes, and taste after each addition. Adding too much could spoil the wine.

ROSEHIP WINE

BEER

Making beer at home is both easy and economical. Since it is not as lengthy a process as wine making, you should be able to sample your efforts within two to three weeks of brewing.

INGREDIENTS

At one time, the sole ingredients of beer were *water*, a *flavouring ingredient, malted barley* and *yeast*. Now *sugar* is frequently added to give extra strength and body.

Water: Most commercial brewers use their own well or spring water. For home brewing use tap water that you have boiled for 1 minute in an open pan.

Flavouring: Until the sixteenth century, various herbs were used both to flavour and preserve beer. Then hops were introduced and were soon adopted universally by the brewing trade. Herbs were still used in country districts where hops were hard to come by. They tend to make light, delicate-flavoured beers which can still be enjoyed today.

Hops also flavour and help to preserve beer and are responsible for the characteristic bitter quality. They can be bought dried from most home brewers' suppliers. The old varieties once favoured by brewers include Goldings, Fuggles and Northern Brewer. Of the newer varieties Challenger, Target and Northdown are the most popular. If a recipe stipulates one variety and you can only obtain another remember that you need approximately *one quarter more of the old varieties than of the new ones*. Dried hops should be a green-gold colour with a fresh smell and slightly resinous texture.

You can also buy hop pellets. The amount needed for a certain quantity of beer or the equivalent in dried hops is usually indicated on the packet.

Malt: Malt is produced by sprouting and then roasting barley grains. The lighter the roast, the lighter the malt and it is the combinations of light and dark malts which give particular flavours and colours to different beers. For home brewing you can buy grain malt or malt extracts.

Grain malt consists of the whole malt grains or ready crushed grains. If you buy the whole grains, you must crush them yourself. To do this, put the malt into a polythene bag. Tie the top loosely and place the bag on a wooden board. Crush the grains with a rolling pin.

A small coffee mill may also be used for crushing malt, although the motor should only be switched on in short bursts so the grains are just broken rather than ground finely. A small hand mincer fitted with a large blade will also do the job effectively.

Black malt grains are usually used whole.

Malt extract is easier to use than grain malt. It comes in the form of a thick, sticky brown syrup. Always use the type that is recommended for brewing rather than that sold in chemists for use as a food supplement.

Other Grains: Flaked barley, flaked maize and oatmeal are occasionally included in both beer and stout recipes. These add extra flavour.

Sugar: Adding sugar to beer increases its alcoholic strength, gives body and helps in the clearing and maturation process. Ordinary granulated sugar will not add colour or flavour to the beer and is often used for light ales. Brown sugars will add both colour and flavour. Demerara is the most suitable for bitter beers and the very dark Barbados or molasses sugars are sometimes used for stout.

Yeast: Buy granulated brewer's yeast from home brew shops.

BEER–MAKING EQUIPMENT

The equipment needed for beer making is simple and economical. Keep it separate from your kitchen equipment; wash it well after use and keep it in a clean cupboard. Before use sterilise it as for wine-making equipment (see page 10).

You will need:

a large stainless steel, aluminium or non-chipped enamel pan for boiling

a white polythene fermentation bin with a tight fitting lid, or a collapsible polypin inside a cardboard carton

plastic stirring spoon

at least 1 metre/1 yard of polythene tubing for siphon

straining bag

beer bottles

screw stoppers or crown caps plus an implement for fitting them

BASIC METHOD FOR MAKING 1 GALLON BEER

1. Boil the hops, malt and sugar in 4.5 litres/1 gallon boiled water for 1–1½ hours.

2. Strain the liquid, now known as the *wort,* into a fermentation bin.

3. Make it up to 4.5 litres/1 gallon with boiled water.

4. Cool to lukewarm.

5. Add the yeast. Either sprinkle it directly onto the wort, or you can sprinkle it into about 150ml/¼ pint of the wort and leave it for 15 minutes or until it begins to froth.

6. Cover, and leave the beer in a warm place for 3 days or until the thick layer of bubbles that first appears on the surface has almost disappeared. This will indicate that the beer has stopped fermenting.

7. Siphon off the beer, leaving the sediment in the bottom of the fermentation bin.

8. Bottle, adding ½ teaspoon sugar per 600ml/1 pint beer. Seal the bottles tightly.

9. Stand the bottles in the cool until the beer clears. This will take about 1 week.

10. When serving, pour out the beer carefully, leaving the sediment in the bottom of the bottles.

BEER KITS

A **dry kit** will contain malt flour, hops and malt grain, plus a sachet of yeast. The hops and malt grain may well be tied in a muslin bag.

Basic Method

1. Dissolve the malt flour and sugar in warm water in a fermentation bin.

2. Put the hops and malt grains into a saucepan with cooled boiled water. Bring them to the boil and simmer for 1 hour.

3. Strain the liquid into the fermentation bin.

Proceed from step 4 above.

A **wet kit** consists of a can of dark brown, thick syrup, which is the concentrated wort. The manufacturers' instructions may vary slightly, but most methods are similar to the following:

1. Put the specified amount of boiling water into a fermentaion bin. Add the wort. Pour a little boiling water into the empty tin to dissolve out any wort that is still clinging to the sides.

2. Add the sugar and stir to dissolve.

3. Add cooled boiled water to the amount given in the kit.

4. Cool to lukewarm.

Proceed from step 5 in the method above.

Additions to wet kits: If you enjoy using one particular kit but feel the flavour could be improved slightly, experiment with extra hops or malt extract.

To give a stronger, more hoppy flavour, use 25g/1oz dried hops for every 11.25 litres/2½ gallons of beer to be made. Boil them with the water for 30 minutes; strain and add the wort while the water is still boiling. Additional malt extract (100g/4oz) can be added with the sugar.

BITTER BEER I
Makes 4.5 litres/1 gallon

15g/½oz dried Golding hops
450g/1lb malt extract
450g/1lb demerara sugar plus 4 teaspoons for
bottling
water
brewer's yeast to make 4.5 litres/1 gallon beer

Boil the hops, malt extract and sugar in 4.5 litres/1 gallon water for 1 hour. Strain the wort into a fermentation bin. Add cooled boiled water to make the amount back up to 4.5 litres/1 gallon. Cool to lukewarm and add the yeast.

Cover and leave in a warm place to ferment for about 3 days, or until fermentation is complete.

Rack off the beer and bottle it, adding ½ teaspoon sugar per 600 ml/1 pint. Cover tightly.

Stand the beer in a cool place for 3 weeks before opening.

BITTER BEER II
Makes 9 litres/2 gallons

450g/1lb malt extract
450g/1lb crushed pale malt
225g/8oz flaked maize
25g/1oz Challenger hops
350g/12oz demerara sugar plus 4 teaspoons for
bottling
9 litres/2 gallons water
brewer's yeast

Heat half the water to 70°C/160°F. Stir in the malt extract, pale malt and flaked maize. Keep at a temperature of 66°C/155°F for 1 hour. Add three-quarters of the hops and boil for 30 minutes. Add the remaining hops and boil for a further 15 minutes.

Put the sugar into a fermentation bin. Strain on the liquid. Add the remaining water cold. Stir to dissolve the sugar. Cover and cool to lukewarm. Sprinkle in

the yeast. Cover and leave in a warm place for 3 days or until fermentation is complete.

Rack off the beer. Bottle it, adding ½ teaspoon sugar per 600 ml/1 pint. Stand the bottles in a cool place for 3 weeks or until the beer is clear.

MILD ALE
Makes 4.5 litres/1 gallon

15g/½oz Fuggles hops
450g/1lb malt extract
450g/1lb sugar plus 4 teaspoons for bottling
4.5 litres/1 gallon water plus extra for topping up
brewer's yeast

Boil the hops, malt extract and sugar in the water for 90 minutes. Add more water to bring the volume back up to 4.5 litres/1 gallon. Strain the liquid into a fermentation bin. Cover and cool to lukewarm.

Sprinkle in the yeast. Cover and keep in a warm place for 3 days or until fermentation is complete.

Rack off the beer and bottle it, adding ½ teaspoon sugar per 600 ml/1 pint. Cover tightly.

Stand the beer in a cool place for 3 weeks before opening.

LIGHT ALE
Makes 4.5 litres/1 gallon

15g/½oz Golding hops
350g/12oz malt extract
225g/8oz sugar plus 4 teaspoons for bottling
4.5 litres/1 gallon water
brewer's yeast

Put the hops into a saucepan with 1.15 litres/2 pints water. Boil them for 30 minutes. Put the malt extract and sugar into a fermentation bin. Strain on the liquid from the hops and stir to dissolve them. Add the remaining water cold. Cool to lukewarm and

sprinkle in the yeast. Cover and leave in a warm place for 3 days or until fermentation is complete.

Rack off the beer and bottle it, adding ½ teaspoon sugar per 600 ml/1 pint. Stand the bottles in a cool place for 2–3 weeks or until the beer is clear.

STOUT
Makes 4.5 litres/1 gallon

40g/1½oz Fuggles hops
100g/4oz black malt grains
450g/1lb demerara sugar plus 4 teaspoons for bottling
water
brewer's yeast to make 4.5 litres/1 gallon stout

Boil the hops, malt grains and sugar in the water for 1 hour. Strain the wort into a fermentation bin and make up to 4.5 litres/1 gallon with boiled water.

Cool to blood heat and add the yeast. Cover and leave in a warm place for 3 days or until fermentation is complete.

Rack and bottle, adding ½ teaspoon sugar per 600 ml/1 pint. Seal tightly.

Stand the bottles in a cool place for 3 weeks before opening.

GINGER BEER
Makes 4.5 litres/1 gallon

25g/1oz root ginger, bruised
450g/1lb sugar
thinly pared rind and juice of 2 lemons
7g/¼oz cream of tartar
4.5 litres/1 gallon boiling water
1 teaspoon brewer's yeast
yeast nutrient

Put the ginger, sugar, lemon rind and cream of tartar into a fermenting bin. Pour on the boiling water. Stir well. Cover and cool to lukewarm.

Add the lemon juice, yeast and yeast nutrient. Cover and leave in a warm place for 3 days.

Strain and put into screw topped bottles. Leave for 4 days before opening. Serve cold.

NETTLE BEER
Makes 4.5 litres/1 gallon

675g/1½lb young nettles
15g/½oz root ginger, bruised
2 lemons
4.5 litres/1 gallon water
450g/1lb demerara sugar plus 4 teaspoons for bottling
25g/1oz cream of tartar
brewer's yeast to make 4.5 litres/1 gallon beer

Put the nettles into a large pan with the ginger, thinly pared lemon rinds and the water. Bring them to the boil and simmer them for 30 minutes.

Put the lemon juice, sugar and cream of tartar into a fermentation bin. Strain on the nettle liquid, pressing down hard on the nettles to extract as much as possible. Make the liquid up to 4.5 litres/1 gallon with boiled water. Stir for the sugar to dissolve.

Cool to lukewarm and add the yeast. Cover and leave to ferment in a warm place for 3 days or until fermentation is complete.

Rack off the beer and bottle it, adding ½ teaspoon sugar per 600ml/1 pint. Seal tightly.

Stand the bottles in a cool place until the beer is clear, about 1 week.

CIDER

The only ingredients essential to a good cider are apples. Left until they have become soft and slightly wrinkled, they are then crushed and pressed; the juice that flows from them is able to ferment naturally to produce a sharp, refreshing drink that is generally slightly more alcoholic than beer. Both sugar and yeast can be added to aid fermentation if wished.

Traditionally, cider has been made from specially grown cider apples. The sweet, bitter and sharp varieties are mixed to achieve the right blend, for example 4 parts sweet, 2 sharp and 1 bitter. Cider apples may not be available to you, but you can obtain a good flavour by mixing dessert and cooking varieties. Add crab apples, if they are available, to provide extra tannin.

To make cider, the apples should be crushed as for wine (see page 14). The juice should then be extracted by either squeezing the pulp in muslin or by putting it through a specially designed press. When making cider it is always the juice that is fermented, not the pulp as in many wine recipes.

On average you will need 9kg/20lb apples to produce 1 gallon juice.

If you find the amount of apples rather overwhelming or if you have no means of pressing and extracting the juice, you can still make an excellent cider using concentrated apple juice. This comes in the form of a sticky brown syrup and can be bought from winemakers' suppliers and from health food shops.

TRADITIONAL CIDER

7.25kg/16lb cooking apples
2.75kg/6lb dessert apples

Leave the apples in a warm place for several weeks or until they are beginning to soften. Crush them to a pulp. Either strain through muslin, squeezing hard, or put them through a commercial press.

Put the juice into a fermentation bin and leave it in a warm place until bubbles have risen to the surface of the liquid and any sediment has sunk to the bottom.

Put the cider into a dark-coloured demijohn. Cover tightly. Leave in a cool place for 6 months.

Siphon the cider into beer bottles. Fit air tight caps. The cider can be consumed straight away.

DRY CIDER

7.25kg/16lb cooking apples
2.75kg/6lb dessert apples
225g/8oz sugar
Champagne yeast
yeast nutrient
1 Campden tablet

Leave the apples in a warm place for several weeks or until they begin to soften. Crush them to a pulp. Either strain through muslin, squeezing hard, or put them through a commercial press.

Put the juice into a demijohn and leave it in a cool place for 24 hours.

Add the yeast and yeast nutrient. Fit a fermentation lock. Leave in a cool place until fermentation is complete, about 3 weeks.

Rack off the cider into a dark-coloured demijohn. Add 1 crushed Campden tablet. Cork tightly. Leave in a cold place until the cider is clear.

Rack off into sealed beer bottles. Store upright in a cold place for 3–4 months.

Medium Sweet Cider

Make as for Dry cider using 900g/2lb sugar.

Sparkling Cider

Make as for Dry cider. Omit the Campden tablet. When bottling, add ½ teaspoon sugar to each 600 ml/1 pint bottle. Use screw-topped bottles or tightly sealed beer bottles.

CIDER WITH RAISINS

4.5 kg/10lb cooking apples
450g/1lb raisins
5 Campden tablets, crushed
4.5 litres/1 gallon water
450g/1lb sugar
Champagne yeast
2 Campden tablets, crushed

Wash and finely chop the apples, using a stainless steel knife. Chop or mince the raisins. Put the apples and raisins into a fermentation bin. Add the Campden tablets.

Dissolve the sugar in the water. Pour it over the apples and raisins. Cover and leave for 3 days, stirring twice a day. Add the yeast. Cover and leave in a warm place for about 2 weeks or until the bubbles cease form.

Strain into a second fermentation bin, squeezing to extract as much liquid as possible. Siphon into a demijohn. Cork tightly and leave in a cool place until the cider is clear.

Put the cider into beer bottles adding ½ teaspoon sugar per 600 ml/1 pint. Seal tightly. Store upright in a cool place for 3 months.

CIDER FROM CONCENTRATED APPLE JUICE

250ml/8fl oz concentrated apple juice
275g/10oz sugar
4.5 litres/1 gallon cold water
all-purpose yeast
1 teaspoon pectin-destroying enzyme

Put all the ingredients into a demijohn. Fit a fermentation lock. Leave for 7–10 days or until fermentation is complete.

Rack off into sealed beer bottles adding ½ teaspoon sugar per pint.

JUICES, SYRUPS AND SQUASHES

When fruit is plentiful at the height of its season, it is well worth making your own juices, syrups and squashes. They will have the fresh, natural flavours of newly picked fruits and can be made without the use of colouring, artificial sweeteners or preservatives.

Fruit juices are made either by pulping and sieving fresh fruits or by steeping them or boiling them in water. The method usually depends on the type of fruit. These fresh juices are best if they are drunk immediately, though they will keep for up to two days in a covered container in the refrigerator.

Fruit syrups are made by adding sugar to fruit juices. Other syrups can be made with nut milks or with herbs and spices. All syrups can be diluted with water or mineral water to make refreshing drinks or used for flavouring in cocktails. Add them to sweet sauces, jellies and puddings, or spoon them over ice cream.

Fruit squashes are usually made with citrus fruits. The rinds are used for flavour and discarded but a little of the flesh is kept in for interest.

EQUIPMENT

vegetable mill (for some juices only)
large polythene or earthenware bowls
large pestle or rolling pin with flat ends
nylon sieves
muslin (or worn, but clean, linen tea towels)
stainless steel or enamel saucepans
large wooden spoons
funnel
small bottles
screw–on caps or corks

Note: Do not use copper, zinc or iron utensils. These spoil colour and flavour and destroy the vitamin C.

FRUIT SYRUPS

Fruit: Soft fruits are mainly used for fruit syrups. They should be ripe (but not overripe) and free of all stalks and leaves. Discard any blemished fruits.

Sugar: Use 350g/12oz sugar to every 600ml/1 pint juice. Ordinary granulated sugar is mostly used as it preserves both the colour and flavour of the fruit. However, brown sugars or honey may be used.

The sugar is added to the cold juice and heated very gently until it has dissolved.

Extracting the juice: Two methods

1. Put the fruit into a large casserole or earthenware bowl with a small amount of water. Stand the container in a large saucepan of water. Set the saucepan on a low heat until the fruit juices begin to run. Cool and strain through muslin.

2. Cold method. This takes longer, but the final syrup has a fresher flavour and more vitamin C is preserved. Put the fruit into a large bowl. Crush it with a wooden pestle or end of a rolling pin. Cover it with clingfilm. Leave it in a warm place until small bubbles begin to appear on the surface. This will take about 24 hours for strawberries and raspberries, up to 3 days for currants and gooseberries. Strain through muslin, squeezing to extract as much juice as possible.

Preserving: The syrup must either be boiled or heat-treated in order to be preserved.

If after the sugar has dissolved the syrup is brought quickly to the boil and then cooled before bottling, it will keep unopened for up to 6 weeks in the refrigerator.

For a shelf life of up to 6 months, the syrup must be heat-processed in the bottles. In this case, there is no need to boil it first. Bottle the syrup, leaving a space of at least 4cm/1½ inches in the top of each bottle. Fit the corks or screw caps only loosely. Stand the bottles on a stand in a saucepan or special water bath. Separate them with wads of newspaper. Pour in cold water to just above the level of the liquid in the bottles. Heat the water to 77°C/170°F and hold it there for 30 minutes. Remove the bottles. Tighten the corks or caps and leave to cool. Store syrups preserved in this way in a cool, dark cupboard.

Bottling: If possible, use small bottles. Screw-topped soft drink bottles are ideal. Wash them well. Place them on the rack in the oven and heat them to 200°C/400°F/Gas 6. Cool them before putting in the syrup. Boil the tops or corks for 5 minutes. Cool them before using.

Labelling: Label bottles with the name of the syrup and the date made.

SQUASHES

Squashes should be preserved and stored in the same way as syrups.

Note: Since fruits vary in their juiciness and ripeness, the amounts of sugar and yields given for some syrups can only be approximate.

TOMATO JUICE
Makes about 750ml/1¼ pints

900g/2lb ripe tomatoes
salt and freshly ground black pepper
300ml/½ pint cold tap water or still mineral
water
juice of up to 1 lemon

Wash the tomatoes. Cut them into 5mm/¼ inch thick wedges. Put them through the fine blade of a vegetable mill.

Season the purée to taste. Gradually stir in the water.

Serve slightly chilled or poured over crushed ice.

Spiced Tomato Juice
Make as above, adding 2–3 tablespoons Worcestershire sauce, or to taste.

Herbed Tomato Juice
Make as above, adding 4 tablespoons chopped fresh chervil, OR 2 tablespoons chopped fresh basil, OR 2 tablespoons each chopped fresh parsley or chives with the lemon juice.

Red Hot Tomato Juice
Make as above, adding 1 teaspoon chilli sauce, or to taste.

PINEAPPLE JUICE
Makes about 900ml/1½ pints

1 large pineapple
juice of ½ lemon
150ml/¼ pint cold tap water or still mineral
water

Cut the husk from the pineapple. Cut the flesh into chunks. Work them to a purée in a food processor or blender. Put the purée into a bowl and stir in the lemon juice. Leave, covered, for 2 hours.

Place a nylon sieve over a second bowl. Ladle in the purée, a little at a time. Press down and stir to allow as much juice as possible to go through into the bowl.

Dilute with water to taste. Serve slightly chilled or poured over crushed ice.

BLACK GRAPE JUICE
Makes about 750 ml/1¼ pints

900g/2lb black grapes
juice of ½ lemon, optional

Halve the grapes and put them into a bowl. Crush them to a rough purée, using a pestle. Cover them and leave them in a cool place for 2 hours, or until the juice has been coloured purple by the skins.

Place a sieve over a bowl. Ladle in the grape purée, a little at a time. Press down hard to allow the juice to drain through, but do not rub through any pieces of skin or flesh.

Taste the juice. Add lemon juice if wished. Chill slightly before serving.

APPLE JUICE
Makes about 2.25 litres/4 pints

1.8kg/4lb dessert apples
juice of 1 lemon
2.25 litres/4 pints boiling water

Cut each apple in half lengthways and then crossways into 3mm/⅛ inch slices. As each apple is cut, put it into a large bowl and toss it in the lemon juice. This will prevent the apples or the subsequent juice from turning brown.

When all the apples are sliced, pour in the water. Cover and leave the apples for 2 hours.

Strain off the juice. Serve at room temperature or slightly chilled.

BLACKCURRANT SYRUP

Makes about 2 litres/3½ pints

1.8kg/4lb blackcurrants
800g/1¾lb sugar (approximately—see Basic method, p. 38)

Wash the blackcurrants. Remove any stalks and leaves. Put the blackcurrants into a bowl and crush them with a pestle or the end of a rolling pin.

Cover and leave them in a warm place until small bubbles begin to form on the surface. this may take up to 3 days.

Put a nylon sieve over a bowl. Line it with muslin. Pour in the blackcurrants. Bring the edges of the muslin together and squeeze to extract as much juice as possible.

Measure the juice and put it into an enamel or stainless steel saucepan. Stir in the required amount of sugar. Set the pan on a very low heat and stir until all the sugar has dissolved. If any pieces of sugar stick round the sides of the pan, push them down with a pastry brush dipped in hot water.

Raise the heat and bring the syrup to the boil. Reduce the heat to low again. Move the pan aside so that it is only half on the heat. Skim away any scum. Take the pan completely from the heat and leave the syrup to cool.

Pour the syrup into bottles. Cork securely or tightly fit a screw cap.

RASPBERRY, REDCURRANT AND HONEY SYRUP

Makes about 2 litres/3½ pints

900g/2lb raspberries
900g/2lb redcurrants
approximately 800g/1¾lb honey (see basic method, p. 38)

Wash the redcurrants and remove the stalks. Put them into a large bowl with the raspberries. Crush them with a large wooden pestle or with the end of a rolling pin.

Cover them with clingfilm and leave them in a warm place until small bubbles form on the surface—24–48 hours.

Put a nylon sieve over a bowl. Line it with muslin. Pour in the fruits. Bring the edges of the muslin together and squeeze to extract as much liquid as possible.

Measure the juice and put it into an enamel or stainless steel saucepan. Stir in the required amount of honey. Set the pan on a very low heat and stir until all the honey has dissolved.

Raise the heat and bring the syrup to the boil. Reduce the heat to low again. Move the pan aside so that it is only half on the heat. Skim away any scum.

Take the pan completely off the heat and leave the syrup to cool completely. Bottle and cork tightly.

MINT SYRUP
Makes about 750 ml/1¼ pints

60 mint leaves
450g/1lb sugar
16fl oz/475 ml water, boiling

Put the mint leaves into a bowl with the sugar. Pound them with a large wooden pestle or with the end of a rolling pin.

Put the sugar and mint leaves into a saucepan. Pour in the boiling water. Stir until the sugar has dissolved. Set the pan on a medium heat and bring the syrup back to the boil. Simmer for 3 minutes to thicken the syrup.

Take the pan from the heat and cool the syrup completely. Pour it into small bottles and cork it or tightly fit screw caps.

FRESH GINGER SYRUP
Makes about 1.75 litres/3 pints

100g/4oz fresh ginger root
1 lemon
1 orange
1.15 litres/2 pints water
900g/2lb demerara sugar

Thinly slice the ginger root. Thinly pare the rinds from the orange and lemon. Squeeze the juices.

Put the ginger, rinds and juices into a saucepan with the water. Bring them to the boil, cover and simmer for 30 minutes. Strain the liquid through a nylon sieve. Measure it. Return it to the pan and make it up to 1.15 litres/2 pints with cold water. Stir in the sugar. Stir on a low heat for it to dissolve. If any pieces of sugar stick round the sides of the pan, push them down with a pastry brush dipped in hot water.

When all the sugar has dissolved, raise the heat and bring the syrup to the boil. Reduce the heat to low again. Move the pan aside so that it is only half on the heat. Skim. Take the pan completely off the heat and leave the syrup to cool completely.

Pour the syrup into small bottles. Cork or tightly fit a screw cap.

COCONUT SYRUP
Makes about 1.75 litres/3 pints

1 large coconut
1.5 litres/2 pints water, boiling
450g/1lb sugar
thinly pared rind and juice of 1 lemon
4½ tablespoons/3fl oz rose-water

Pierce the "eyes" of the coconut. Pour out and reserve the juice. Break the coconut. Take out the flesh and cut away the brown outer skin.

Grate the flesh and put it into a bowl. Pour on the boiling water. Add the juice. Cover and leave for 1 hour.

Place a nylon sieve over a bowl. Line it with muslin. Pour in the coconut and the liquid. Bring the sides of the muslin together and squeeze hard to extract as much liquid as possible. Measure the liquid.

Put the coconut milk into a saucepan. Stir in the sugar. Add the lemon rind and juice and the rose-water. Stir on a low-heat until all the sugar has dissolved. Bring the liquid to the boil. Remove it from the heat. Remove the lemon rind and leave the syrup to cool completely.

Pour the syrup into small bottles. Cork or tightly fit new screw caps.

ORANGE SQUASH
Makes about 1.4 litres/2½ pints

8 large oranges
900ml/1½ pints water
1.25kg/2½lb sugar
25g/1oz citric acid

Thinly pare the rinds from the oranges. Put them into a saucepan with the water. Bring them to the boil and simmer for 5 minutes. Strain the liquid and return it to the pan.

Strain the juice from the oranges. Add it to the saucepan with some of the smaller pieces of the orange pulp. Add the sugar. Set the pan on a low heat and stir for the sugar to dissolve. Add the citric acid. Bring the squash to the boil. Take it immediately from the heat and cool completely.

Pour the squash into small bottles and cork or tightly fit screw caps.

GRAPEFRUIT AND HONEY SQUASH

Makes about 1.4 litres/2½ pints

5 grapefruit
900ml/1½ pints water
900g/2lb honey
25g/1oz citric acid

Thinly pare the rinds from two grapefruit. Put them into a saucepan with the water. Bring them to the boil and simmer for 5 minutes. Strain the liquid and return it to the pan.

Strain the juice from the grapefruit. Add it to the saucepan with some of the smaller pieces of the grapefruit pulp. Add the honey. Set the pan on a low heat and stir until the honey has dissolved. Add the citric acid. Bring the squash to the boil. Take it immediately from the heat and cool it completely.

Pour the squash into small bottles and cork or tightly fit screw caps.

LEMONADE

3 lemons
50g/2oz brown or white sugar OR honey
1.15 litres/2 pints water, boiling

Grate the rinds from the lemons and put them into a large jug or bowl. Cut away and discard all the white pith. Thinly slice the flesh and put it into the jug or bowl.

Pour on the boiling water. Add the sugar or honey and stir. Leave the lemonade until it is completely cold.

Serve slightly chilled, either strained or poured directly from the jug.

Store in the refrigerator for up to 2 days.

LEMON BARLEY WATER

50g/2oz pearl barley
1.4 litres/2½ pints water
3 lemons
50g/2oz brown or white sugar OR honey

Put the pearl barley into a saucepan with the water. Bring them to the boil, cover and simmer for 20 minutes. Strain the liquid and discard the barley.

Meanwhile prepare the lemons as for lemonade. Pour the hot barley water over them and proceed as for lemonade.

BERRY VINEGAR

Makes about 350ml/12fl oz

675g/1½lb raspberries, strawberries OR blackberries, preferably in 225g/8oz amounts every four days
one 375–ml/13–fl oz bottle of white wine vinegar
equal weight of strained vinegar in sugar or honey (225–350g/8–12oz)

Put 225g/8oz berries into a bowl with the vinegar. Cover with kitchen paper or a clean tea towel and leave in a warm place for 4 days. Strain the vinegar and put in a further 225g/8oz berries. Leave for four days. Repeat the process again.

Weigh a bowl. Strain the vinegar through a jelly bag into the bowl. Weigh again. Put the vinegar into a saucepan and put in an equal amount of sugar and honey. Set the pan on a low heat and stir until the sugar has dissolved. Bring the vinegar to the boil. Boil for 5 minutes, skimming well.

Pour the vinegar into an earthenware jug and cover it with a linen tea towel, folded into four. Tie the cloth down securely and leave the vinegar for 24 hours.

Pour the vinegar back into the original bottle and screw on the top. It will keep for up to a year but can be used imediately.

Dilute with either hot or cold water for a fresh-tasting drink, or use it in sauces for sweet and savoury dishes.

CORDIALS

Cordials were originally spirit-based drinks flavoured with fruits and spices and often coloured. They were served diluted with hot water, mainly for medicinal purposes.

Although the word came to refer to any sweetened, fruit-based drink, the recipes below are more of the old-fashioned type. The whisky and brandy cordials make delicious, warming winter drinks at any time. The blackberry cordial and elderberry rob are reputed to be cold cures and make excellent bedtime drinks.

Use dark bottles for cordials and store them in a cool, dark cupboard.

LEMON AND BRANDY CORDIAL

Makes about 1.25 litres/2¼ pints

2 lemons
1 bottle brandy (775 ml/26fl oz)
450ml/¾ pint water
225g/8 oz demerara OR granulated sugar
5 cm/2-inch cinnamon stick
2 blades mace
4 cloves
1 nutmeg

Thinly pare the rinds from the lemons. Cut away and discard the pith. Chop the flesh.

Pour off and reserve about one quarter of the brandy from the bottle. Put the lemon rinds and flesh into the bottle, pouring out more brandy if necessary. If the bottle is not quite full, top up with the reserved brandy. Keep any brandy left over in a covered container. Put the top back on the brandy bottle and leave the brandy in a cool place for 3 days. Strain off the brandy into a large bowl.

Put the water into a saucepan with the sugar and spices. Stir on a low heat for the sugar to dissolve. Boil the syrup for 5 minutes. Take it from the heat and cool it completely. Strain the syrup into the brandy. Add the reserved brandy. Stir well. Bottle.

Serve diluted one part to five with hot water.

WHISKY AND REDCURRANT CORDIAL

Makes about 1 litre/1¾ pints

350g/12oz redcurrants, fresh or frozen
thinly pared rind of 2 lemons
15g/½oz fresh ginger root, peeled and grated
1 bottle whisky
350g/12oz sugar or honey

Remove any stalks and leaves from the redcurrants. Put them into a bowl with the lemon rind and ginger root. Pour in the whisky. Cover with clingfilm and leave for 24 hours.

Strain the whisky through a nylon sieve into another bowl. Stir in the sugar or honey. Cover with clingfilm again. Leave for 12 hours.

Pour the cordial into bottles. Put on tight screw caps or cork.

Serve as Lemon and brandy cordial (left).

BLACKBERRY CORDIAL

Makes about 1.75 litres/3 pints

2.75kg/6lb blackberries
1 tablespoon allspice berries
1 tablespoon cloves
7.5-cm/3-inch cinnamon stick
2 nutmegs
4½ tablespoons/3fl oz water
350g/12oz honey OR sugar to each 600ml/1 pint liquid
200ml/7fl oz brandy

Put the blackberries into a large pan with the spices and water. Bring them gently to the boil and cook them until they are very juicy, about 20 minutes.

Line a large bowl with muslin or a worn but clean tea towel. Pour the blackberries through it. Squeeze hard to extract as much juice as possible. Measure the juice and return it to the cleaned pan.

Bring the juice to the boil. Add the honey or sugar. Boil for 10 minutes. Take the pan from the heat and wait for the syrup to stop bubbling. Pour in the brandy. Pour the cordial into hot, sterilised bottles and cork tightly. To serve, dilute one part to four with hot water.

ELDERBERRY ROB

Makes about 1.15 litres/2 pints

1.8kg/4lb elderberries, weighed on the stem
two 5-cm/2-inch cinnamon sticks
1 piece dried root ginger, bruised
2 nutmegs
1 teaspoon allspice berries
1 teaspoon cloves
300ml/½ pint water
350g/12oz honey or sugar to each 600ml/1 pint liquid
150ml/¼ pint brandy

Take the elderberries from the stalks. Put them into a saucepan with the spices and water. Bring them gently to the boil and simmer for about 20 minutes or until the pan is full of juice.

Place a piece of muslin or a worn but clean linen tea towel over a large bowl. Pour the elderberries through it. Gather the sides together and squeeze out as much juice as you can. Measure it and return it to the cleaned saucepan.

Bring the juice to the boil and add the honey or sugar. Stir for it to dissolve and then boil the syrup for 10 minutes. Take the pan from the heat and wait until the syrup stops bubbling. Pour in the brandy.

Pour the hot cordial into hot, sterilised bottles and cork it tightly. Store in a cool, dark place.

To serve, dilute one part to four with hot water.

MILK DRINKS

Milk makes nourishing drinks, both hot and cold, which can be served as thirst quenchers, as desserts, or even as a quick meal in themselves.

Milk drinks can vary in their richness. They can be given just one simple flavouring, or thickened with eggs or ice cream. Whipped cream can be spooned over the top.

Yoghurt can be made into refreshing cold drinks that are particularly welcome in the summer. The simplest yoghurt drink is known as *Ayran* and consists of equal parts of yoghurt and chilled water, mixed and poured over crushed ice. Ayran can be given either sweet or savoury flavours and so can be served either as a dessert or as an appetiser.

Buttermilk has recently become more available and can be bought in some supermarkets. It is thinner than yoghurt with a similar, refreshing flavour. It can be drunk straight from the carton or diluted and flavoured.

PEAR AND APPLE SHAKE
Makes 4 drinks

740ml/1 ¼ pints milk
4 tablespoons pear and apple spread★
8 tablespoons vanilla ice cream
1 dessert apple
juice of ½ lemon

Put the milk into a large blender with 3 tablespoons of the pear and apple spread and half the ice cream. Blend until the spread has become well incorporated with the milk.

Pour the shake into four tall glasses. Float 1 tablespoon ice cream on each one. Top it with a small portion of the remaining spread.

Core the apple and cut it into thin, lengthways slices. Toss the slices in the lemon juice. Make a small slit near the top of each slice to hang them over the rims of the glasses.

★ Pear and apple spread is a thick, sweet brown syrup made from the concentrated juices of pears and apples. It can be bought from most health food shops.

RASPBERRY ICE CREAM SODA
Makes 4 drinks

225g/8oz raspberries, fresh or frozen, plus extra for garnish
50g/2oz sugar or honey
8 tablespoons vanilla ice cream
900ml/1½ pints soda water or sparkling mineral water
5 tablespoons/3½fl oz double cream, whipped (optional)

Rub the raspberries through a sieve. Stir the sugar or honey into the resulting purée. Put a portion of the sweetened purée into the bottom of four tall glasses.

Put half the ice cream into a large blender with the soda or mineral water. Blend well. Pour the blended mixture over the raspberry purée.

Float a further tablespoon of ice cream on top of each glass. Spoon the cream over the top, if desired. Garnish with whole raspberries.

HOT CAROB MILK WITH VANILLA ISLANDS

Makes 4 drinks

75g/3oz sugar-free carob bars (two small bars)★
4 tablespoons water
900ml/1½ pints milk
6 tablespoons/4fl oz double cream
¼ teaspoon vanilla essence

Break up the carob bars and put them into a saucepan with the water. Put the milk into a separate saucepan. Whip the cream with the vanilla essence until it will stand up in peaks.

Set the carob bars on a low heat and stir until they melt and become thick and smooth. Do not overheat or the carob will become grainy in texture. In another pan, heat the milk to just below boiling point. Pour it into the carob, a little at a time, stirring well. Whisk on a low heat for 5 minutes without letting the mixture boil.

Pour the drink into four cups. Float the vanilla flavoured cream on the top.

★ Sugar-free carob bars can be bought from most health food shops, their flavour similar to that of dark chocolate. Ordinary plain chocolate may be used instead.

PEPPERMINT YOGHURT COOLER

Makes 4 drinks

450ml/¾ pint natural yoghurt, chilled
¼ teaspoon peppermint essence
few drops green food colouring
3 tablespoons sugar OR honey
450ml/¾ pint cold water or still mineral water, chilled
crushed ice (p. 50)
grated rind of 1 lemon
8 cucumber slices

Put the natural yoghurt into a bowl. Add the peppermint essence, food colouring and sugar or honey. Stir until the sugar or honey has dissolved. Gradually stir in the water to make a smooth mixture.

Quarter fill four tall glasses with crushed ice. Pour in the yoghurt drink. Grate a little lemon rind over the top. Hang two cucumber slices on the edge of each glass.

BUTTERMILK AND LEMON FIZZ

Makes 4 drinks

450ml/¾ pint cultured buttermilk, chilled
grated rind and juice of 2 lemons
4 teaspoons sugar or honey
450ml/¾ pint soda water or sparkling mineral water
4 slices lemon
mint sprigs, optional

Put the buttermilk into a jug. Grate in the lemon rinds. Put the lemon juice into a small bowl. Add the sugar or honey and stir until it dissolves. Stir the mixture into the buttermilk. Pour in the soda or mineral water.

Pour the drink into four tall glasses. Garnish with lemon slices and mint sprigs.

COCKTAILS AND APERITIFS

A cocktail consists of a spirit or liqueur, iced and mixed with flavourings such as fruit juice of syrup. Most cocktails should be served before dinner although some are designed to be served after a meal. The variety of cocktails from all over the world is so great (not to mention colourful and delicious) that this book cannot show them all. Hence the most popular are included here; they are simple to make and in general use easily obtainable ingredients.

INGREDIENTS

Ice: Ice is used both to chill and to slightly dilute cocktails. If only a slight dilution is required, ice cubes are used. Crushed ice will give added texture to a cocktail, besides more dilution.

Generally, the ingredients of the cocktail are shaken or stirred with the ice before being strained into a glass. More ice can be added in the glass if wished.

When making ice, avoid placing food near it in the freezer or freezing compartment of the refrigerator since food may contaminate it with a strong smell. Ice cubes can be made in advance and stored in polythene bags in the freezer.

To crush ice, either work ice cubes in a blender or food processor, or place them between two folded towels and crush them with a wooden mallet. Crushed ice can also be stored in the freezer.

Fruits Juices and Peels: Where only small amounts of fruit juice are required your cocktail will have a better flavour if they are freshly squeezed. Where larger amounts are needed, such as in the Tequila sunrise, it will be more convenient to use bought juice. This should be natural and unsweetened. Frozen, concentrated orange juice gives a better flavour than bottled or cartoned.

Fruit peel for garnish or for flavour must be very thinly pared with a vegetable peeler. To extract as much flavour as possible, squeeze the peel in your fingers before putting it into the glass.

EQUIPMENT

Measures: All the recipes below use the standard cocktail measure, also known as a jigger. It holds 45ml/1½fl oz or 2½ tablespoons. Measures are cheap to buy and very useful if you make cocktails frequently.

Cocktail Shaker: Cocktail shakers come in varying shapes and sizes but all have the same function. The spirit and liqueur ingredients for cocktails have different densities and so would separate if not mixed thoroughly. In a shaker they can be both mixed together and chilled with ice. A good shaker should have a strainer attachment so the drink and not the ice can be poured out.

Mixing Glass: Some cocktails are stirred rather than shaken. Use any 300ml/½ pint tumbler for this and transfer the cocktail to another glass for stirring.

Mixing Spoon: You need a teaspoon with a very long handle.

Ice Equipment: Some means of crushing (see above—a bowl for holding the used ice from the shaker; an ice bucket and tongs).

Cocktail Sticks: These hold cherries, olives, etc. for garnish.

Drinking Glasses: There were once standard shapes for cocktail glasses, but there is now an extremely wide variety available, some even with built-in straws. The traditional cocktail glass is stemmed, with the sides sloping outwards, and has a capacity of 60–125ml/2–4fl oz. An old-fashioned glass is short and chubby, again with the sides sloping outwards. A whisky glass is a short, narrow, straight-sided tumbler and a whisky sour glass is tall, stemmed and tulip shaped. Longer drinks are served in straightforward tumblers.

Note: Each recipe below is for **one** drink.

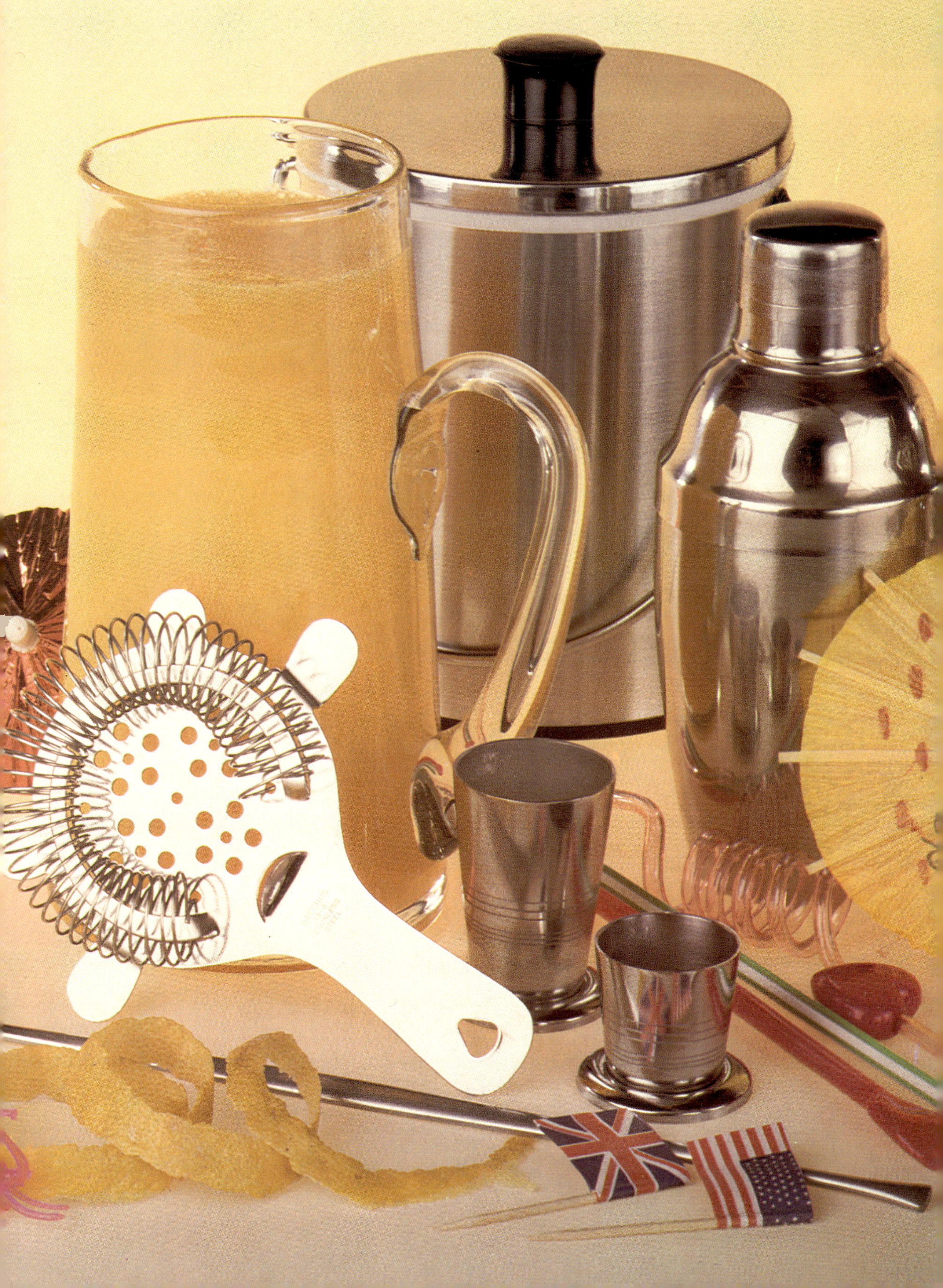

MANHATTAN

2 measures Bourbon whisky
½ measure sweet vermouth
dash Angostura bitters
3 ice cubes
garnish
1 strip orange peel
1 maraschino cherry

Put all the ingredients into a cocktail shaker. Shake well and strain into a chilled cocktail glass. Garnish with the orange peel and cherry.

MANHATTAN DRY

½ measure dry vermouth
2 measures Bourbon whisky
4 ice cubes
garnish
1 strip lemon peel
1 green olive, stoned

Put the vermouth, whisky and ice into a mixing glass. Stir gently. Strain into a cocktail glass. Garnish with the lemon peel and olive.

WHISKY SOUR

2 measures Bourbon whisky
juice of ½ lemon
1 teaspoon caster sugar
4 ice cubes
garnish:
1 strip orange peel
1 cocktail cherry

Put the Bourbon, lemon juice and sugar into a cocktail shaker and stir to dissolve the sugar. Add the ice cubes. Put on the lid and shake well.

Place the orange peel and cherry in a chilled whisky sour glass. Strain in the cocktail.

WHISKY SOUR COCKTAIL

2 measures Bourbon whisky
1 tablespoon orange juice
1 tablespoon lemon juice
2 teaspoons caster sugar
3 ice cubes, crushed
soda water OR sparkling mineral water
garnish:
1 slice lemon and 1 slice orange
2 maraschino cherries

Put the whisky, juices, sugar and ice into a cocktail shaker. Shake well and strain into a tall glass.

Garnish with the orange and lemon slices and cherries. Serve with a straw.

MARTINI DRY

2 measures gin
1 measure dry vermouth
4 ice cubes
1 strip lemon rind
garnish:
1 stuffed olive

Put the gin, vermouth and ice cubes into a cocktail shaker. Shake well. Rub the rim of a chilled cocktail glass with the cut side of the lemon rind. Strain in the martini.

Garnish with the olive.

MARTINI SWEET

2 measures gin
1 measure sweet vermouth
garnish:
1 strip orange peel
1 maraschino cherry

Pour the gin and vermouth into a chilled cocktail glass. Stir. Garnish with the orange peel and cherry.

PINK GIN (GIN AND BITTERS)

dash Angostura bitters
2 measures gin
1 ice cube

Put the Angostura bitters into a cocktail glass. Swirl it round to coat the inside of the glass. The bitters can then be shaken out of the glass or left in for more flavour and colour.

Pour in the gin. Add the ice cube.

Note: The gin may be diluted with iced water or soda water, if wished.

PINK GIN AND TONIC

Make Pink gin as above, using a tall glass. Top up with tonic. Add an ice cube and garnish with a slice of lemon, if wished.

WHITE LADY

1 measure gin
½ measure Cointreau
1 tablespoon lemon juice
4 ice cubes, crushed
garnish:
1 slice orange
3 maraschino cherries

Put the gin, Cointreau, lemon juice and ice cubes into a cocktail shaker. Shake well. Strain the mixture into a chilled cocktail glass.

Cut the orange slice in half. Skewer it on a cocktail stick between the cherries.

SCREWDRIVER

2 measures vodka
2 measures orange juice
1 teaspoon icing sugar, optional
4 ice cubes
garnish:
slices of orange

If using the icing sugar, put the vodka and orange juice into a cocktail shaker. Add the icing sugar and shake well. Put the ice cubes into a cocktail glass and strain the mixture.

If the icing sugar is to be omitted, pour first the vodka and then the orange juice over the ice cubes.

BLOODY MARY

12 ice cubes
1 measure vodka
2 measures tomato juice
2 teaspoons lemon juice
½ teaspoon Worcestershire sauce
2 drops Tabasco sauce
freshly ground black pepper
celery salt, optional
garnish:
1 strip lemon peel
1 tomato wedge

Put 8 ice cubes into a cocktail shaker. Pour in the vodka and tomato juice. Add the lemon juice, Worcestershire and Tabasco, and grind in a little pepper. Shake well. Put the remaining ice cubes into a whisky glass and pour in the cocktail.

Sprinkle a little celery salt over the top. Garnish with the lemon peel and tomato wedge.

TEQUILA SUNRISE

1½ measures tequila
3 measures orange juice
8 ice cubes
½ measure grenadine
garnish:
1 orange slice
2 maraschino cherries

Shake the tequila and orange juice with 4 of the ice cubes. Strain them into a tall glass. Float more ice cubes on top.

Slowly pour in the grenadine. Allow to settle. Garnish with the orange slice and cherries. Serve with straws.

HARVEY WALLBANGER

2 measures vodka
4 measures orange juice
4 ice cubes
½ measure Galliano
garnish:
orange slices

Shake the vodka and orange juice together. Put the ice cubes into a glass and pour in the vodka and orange.

Pour the Galliano over the back of a teaspoon onto the vodka and orange. Garnish with orange slices and serve with straws.

BETWEEN THE SHEETS

1 measure brandy
1 measure light rum
1 measure Cointreau
1 tablespoon lemon juice
4 ice cubes

Put all the ingredients into a cocktail shaker and shake well. Strain into a chilled cocktail glass.

Serve after dinner.

FLOATING BRANDY

crushed ice
1 measure crème de menthe
1 tablespoon brandy

Fill a 6 tablespoons/4 fl oz glass with crushed ice. Pour in the crème de menthe. Carefully pour in the brandy over the back of a teaspoon so that it floats on the top.

Serve after dinner.

TOMATO AND TEQUILA COCKTAIL

1 measure tequila
2 measures tomato juice
2 measures freshly squeezed orange juice
¼ teaspoon Tabasco sauce
4 ice cubes
crushed ice
garnish:
1 slice orange
2 wedges tomato

Shake together the tequila, tomato juice, orange juice, Tabasco and ice cubes.

Half fill a tall glass with crushed ice and pour in the cocktail. Garnish with orange slice and wedges of tomato.

PLANTER'S PUNCH

juice of ½ lime
1 teaspoon Barbados sugar
2 measures dark rum
crushed ice
garnish:
2 slices lime
1 maraschino cherry
1 mint sprig

Put the lime juice into a large, tall glass. Add the sugar and stir well for it to dissolve. Add the rum.

Three–quarters fill the glass with the crushed ice and stir. Garnish with the lime, maraschino cherry and mint sprig.

FOAMING DAIQUIRI

2 measures light rum
½ measure lime or lemon juice
2 teaspoons Cointreau
1 teaspoon icing sugar
4 ice cubes
1 teaspoon egg white

Put the rum, lemon or lime juice, Cointreau, icing sugar, ice cubes and egg white into a cocktail shaker. Shake well and strain into a cocktail glass.

Garnish with slices of lime or lemon, if wished.

FRAPPÉ

Fill a cocktail glass with crushed ice. Slowly pour in a liqueur until all the crushed ice is coloured.

The brightly coloured ones such as crème de menthe, parfait d'amour or blue Curacao are extremely effective.

Serve after dinner.

POUSSE-CAFÉ

Pousse-café is an after dinner mixture of liqueurs poured into a glass in descending order of density so that instead of mixing they float on top of each other. It is generally served with coffee.

½ measure crème de cacao
½ measure parfait d'amour
½ measure crème de menthe
½ measure maraschino
½ measure cognac

Pour each liqueur over the back of a teaspoon into a liqueur glass. Serve with a straw. The layers should be drunk separately.

COLD CUPS AND PUNCHES

Originally punches were made from spirits, water, spices, sugar and lemon or lime juice, and were served hot or cold. They have been elaborated and changed over the years and are now made with many different combinations of wines, fruit juices and diced fruit.

To obtain flavour from the fruit, it is very often soaked in all or part of the alcoholic content of the punch before the drink is finally completed. It may be strained off and discarded or served in the glasses with the drink. In this case, use small fruits or finely dice larger ones.

Where the punch is to be served chilled instead of at room temperature, chill the wine before adding it to the rest of the ingredients. If ice is added, remember that it will dilute the punch as it melts. If you do not wish this to happen, use ice cubes and add them just before serving, except in Sangria, in which the dilution is part of the recipe. An alternative to using ice cubes is to place a large chunk of ice or water or fruit juice frozen in a ring mould or attractive jelly mould in the punch bowl with the fruits and to pour wine over it. Your punch then looks as good as it tastes. Crushed ice may be used for stronger mixtures; it should be placed in the glasses and the punch poured on top.

Use pretty glasses for summer punches and chill them slightly before they are filled.

SANGRIA
Serves 6–8

1 litre/1¾ pints dry red wine
3 lemons
25g/1oz sugar, optional
4½ tablespoons/3fl oz brandy
1 lemon
1 orange
2 red-skinned apples
1 ripe pear
4 fresh apricots, if available
2 peaches, if available
24 ice cubes
1 banana
pinch cinnamon

Put the wine into a large bowl with the juice of 2 lemons. Add the sugar and stir until it dissolves.

Thinly slice the remaining lemon. Cut the rind and pith from the orange and chop the flesh. Core and finely chop the apples and pear. Scald, skin and dice the apricots and peaches.

Put all this fruit into the wine. Add the brandy and ice. Cover and leave until the ice has melted. Thinly slice the banana and add it with the cinnamon just

before serving; Sangria should be served in chilled glasses. The fruit may be served in the same glasses or left until the end and served separately.

SUMMER WINE CUP
Serves 4

100g/40oz raspberries OR small strawberries
4½ tablespoons/3fl oz brandy
1 bottle (70cl) dry white wine
½ cucumber, thinly sliced
ice cubes optional

Put the raspberries or strawberries into a large bowl. Pour in the brandy and leave them for 30 minutes. Pour in the wine and add the cucumber slices. Leave for a further 10 minutes.

Serve in chilled glasses, garnished with extra cucumber slices if wished.

SPARKLING CUP
Serves 4

1 bottle (70cl) sparkling white wine
4 large oranges
6 tablespoons/4fl oz medium sherry
4 mint sprigs
crushed ice

Squeeze the juice from 2 of the oranges and thinly slice the other two. Put the juice and the sliced oranges into a bowl. Add the sherry and mint sprigs. Cover and leave for 1 hour.

Strain the liquid into a serving jug. Add the wine. Serve poured over crushed ice (page 50).

ICED TEA PUNCH
Serves 4–6

3 tablespoons Indian tea leaves
125g/4oz honey
4 mint sprigs
4 lemons
6 tablespoons/4fl oz whisky
600 ml/1 pint boiling water
600 ml/1 pint sparkling mineral water, chilled

Put the tea leaves, honey, mint sprigs and the juice of 2 lemons into a jug. Pour on the boiling water. Cover and leave until quite cold. Strain off the liquid and chill it.

Pour the liquid into a bowl. Add the remaining lemons, sliced, the whisky and mineral water.

MULLED DRINKS AND TODDIES

Wines, beers, spirits and cider can all be heated, sweetened, and sometimes diluted to make heady drinks for winter parties or a nightcap for just one person. The main flavouring ingredients are fresh fruits and spices which are heated with the liquids to extract their flavour. Once the punch has been flavoured, the fruit may be strained off or left in to give an attractive appearance.

For heating the punch, choose a large saucepan. Enamel or stainless steel are best, but aluminium can be used provided the drink does not stay in it for any length of time after heating.

No alcoholic beverage should ever be boiled since boiling causes all the alcohol to evaporate. Heat it instead to simmering point and hold it there for 10–20 minutes. Spirits or liqueurs should be added after the wine and other ingredients have been heated so they maintain their maximum strength.

Traditionally all mulled drinks are served from large bowls. If you do not own a punch bowl, a pyrex or earthenware mixing bowl will serve as well. Warm it before you pour in the punch by pouring very hot water into it.

To prevent burned fingers, you should serve mulled drinks in glasses or mugs with handles.

Where a single drink such as the toddy or grog is made in the glass with boiling water, always heat the glass first and stand a metal spoon in it while the water is being poured in. This will prevent the glass from breaking.

HOT TODDY
Serves 1

1 strip lemon peel
1 clove
pinch cinnamon
½ teaspoon honey OR sugar
4½ tablespoons/3fl oz whisky
6 tablespoons/4fl oz boiling water

Warm a tall glass. Lightly squeeze the lemon peel and stick the clove into it. Put it into the glass. Add the honey or sugar, stirring with a long spoon to dissolve it. Leave the spoon in the glass. Pour in the boiling water and stir.

GROG
Serves 1

1 thick lemon slice
2 cloves
1 teaspoon Barbados OR molasses sugar
2.5cm/1-inch cinnamon stick
4½ tablespoons/3fl oz dark rum
6 tablespoons/4fl oz boiling water

Stick the cloves into the lemon slice. Warm a tall glass. Put in the sugar and cinnamon stick into a tall glass. Pour in the rum and stir with a long spoon for the sugar to dissolve. Leave the spoon in the glass.

Put in the lemon slice. Pour in the water. Stir briefly before drinking.

MULLED RED WINE

1 bottle (70cl) dry red wine
1 piece dried ginger root, bruised
5–cm/2–inch cinnamon stick
10 cloves
6 allspice berries
2 dessert apples
2 oranges, sliced
150ml/¼ pint brandy

Put all the ingredients except the brandy into a large saucepan. Bring them to simmering point and keep them there for 15 minutes. Add the brandy and immediately take the pan from the heat.

Strain the wine if wished. Pour it into a warmed bowl and serve as soon as possible.

MEAD PUNCH
Serves 6

1 bottle (70cl) mead
250ml/8fl oz sweet sherry
600ml/1 pint apple juice
2 oranges
12 cloves
13–cm/5–inch cinnamon stick
50g/2oz honey
6 tablespoons/4fl oz whisky

Pour the mead and sherry into a saucepan. Thickly slice the oranges and stick the cloves into the slices. Put them into the saucepan with the cinnamon stick. Add the honey.

Bring the mixture to just below simmering point and hold it there for 20 minutes.

Add the brandy and serve immediately.

LAMBSWOOL
Serves 4–6

10 cooking apples
3 tablespoons Barbados sugar
2.25 litres/4 pints brown ale
15g/½oz dried ginger root, bruised
½ nutmeg, grated
½ teaspoon ground cinnamon

Heat the oven to 200°C/40°F/Gas 6. Core the apples and put them into a shallow, ovenproof dish. Pour in a little water. Bake them for 20 minutes. Sieve the apple pulp and mix it with the sugar.

Put the apple pulp into a saucepan. Stir in the brown ale. Add the ginger, nutmeg and cinnamon. Bring the mixture to simmering point and hold it there for 15 minutes.

Pour the mixture, without sieving, into a warmed bowl and serve immediately.

INDEX